Consumers and Social Services

*I'm having trouble getting my little boy into
school. He had measles when he was small and has
been slow since but he needs to learn. The school
keeps putting me off . . . .*

*I need help with my back rent. I haven't worked
full-time for five months since I was hit by a car.
I lost my job for not reporting in every day and
I couldn't get unemployment compensation. . . .*

*My son is a wanderer. He's 8. He left home nine
or ten times and the police found him three times.
I've kept him in the house, I took away his
special treats, I've beaten him. And he steals,
mostly from me . . . .*

from records of
The Roxbury Multi-Service Center

Consumers
and Social Services

Robert Perlman

Brandeis University

With the technical assistance of

Wyatt C. Jones

Brandeis University

John Wiley & Sons, Inc.

New York   London   Sydney   Toronto

To my parents

Library of Congress Cataloging in Publication Data

Perlman, Robert.
  Consumers and social services.

  1. Social Service. I. Title.
HV41.P45   362   74-13540
ISBN 0-471-68062-1
ISBN 0-471-68064-8 (pbk.)

Printed in the United States of America

10 9 8 7 6 5 4 3 2 1

Foreword

Since their inception, social welfare institutions in the United States have sought a logic and a frame of reference that could encompass humanitarian impulses, the infinite variety of human distress, and the social demand for effectiveness. From the early days of the Association for Improving the Conditions of the Poor in the 1840s and the Chairty Organization Society in the 1880s to the Multipurpose Centers of the 1960s, a continuous search can be traced for some generic and comprehensive framework. The theoretical base for this evolution was weak and ambiguous at best. Political and economic reform movements concentrated on the basic institutions of the social and economic order. Distressed groups, families, or individuals were left to succoring activities guided by religious, humanitarian, psychological, or philanthropic points of view.

These viewpoints produced a succession of specific purpose activities that, over time, accumulated to form the present network of thousands of social welfare organizations. Periodically major efforts were launched to revitalize or to improve the help-giving system. These efforts sometimes took the form of a push toward consolidation of effort, of which the multipurpose center is a recent example. Consolidation or coordination sought to recapture a sense of unity, of coherence, of completeness from a reality made up of discontinuous fragments of humanitarian effort.

In the 1960s and 1970s the dissatisfactions with the existing patterns erupted once again into a major effort to test new patterns and to reconstruct the social services system. Despite vast programs and expenditures through retirement, disability, unemployment, and health insurance, through economic or social development programs and through financial assistance for the poor, problems remained unresolved. Were they due to correctable flaws in these vast payment programs, or to the existence of a not yet defined social difficulty or set of difficulties that demanded yet another system of helping altogether?

In addition to the now accepted human services of income maintenance, health, education, and housing, do we need an additional service system called the personal social services, which has its roots in the historical philanthropic and charitable efforts of the past? The answer seems to be "yes," but the nature of the new system remains vague.

Better answers depend upon better understanding of the nature of the transaction that takes place between users of the social or human services and the providers. Only through close observation and study can ideology or philosophical viewpoints about the nature of human distress be refined into effective activity. Unfortunately, until the recent period, most studies of client-helper transactions have been carried out by the providers themselves.

Inevitably, they have defined the terms of effectiveness within the boundaries of the helper's perception about the nature of human need—is it interpersonal, intrapsychic, social, economic, situational, or environmental?

Doctor Perlman's study of consumers and social services brings the subject to a new level of objectivity, in which value biases are confronted and the empirical reality is examined in an open-minded quest for the reality of the exchange that takes place between person and institution. Viewing the service user as a consumer rather than as a client encourages a fresh look at what goes on between the seeker and the helper. New possibilities are opened up and new questions are also encountered.

Whether called client or consumer, the fact remains that both seeker and helper depend equally upon each. Agencies and professional helpers who cannot attract users or clients or consumers cannot long survive. At one time the state of being a client was involuntary—the person needing help was in fact helpless and the sources of help sharply limited. In the present era, except for small children and legally detained persons such as criminals and the mentally ill, users are the beneficiaries of an entirely new state of affairs. There are a bewildering variety of helping programs and the user's voice is now amplified by advocates, consumer organizations, legal appeals, and the like.

If the client-helper transaction is now viewed as a marketplace operation, which the term 'consumer' implies, then we do face a new opportunity to construct a social service system that may bear little resemblance to the past. If professional helpers accept the marketplace, it follows that what they give will be determined not by professional considerations or ideology alone, but also by demand. It is true that social agencies can influence the market by selling campaigns and by image-building, much as do automobile and cosmetic and refrigerator manufacturers. But in the end the survival of the helping systems, or of their professions, will depend on how well they can perceive the expressible wants of consumers and how ready they are to meet those wants.

Therefore, what consumers expect from their providers or helpers becomes a vital part of the transaction equation. In other words, grating as it is upon professional nerve ends, how well will service agencies "sell" what they perceive to be the wants of clients? The Perlman formulation of consumer groups into problem-solvers, resource seekers and the buffeted is helpful, even if it does not remain the final classification, for it begins to identify consumer wants in psychosocial terms and does not limit us to the provider's view of what the consumer "needs."

Yet this is only the beginning of the journey. No matter how consumers and their wants are grouped, shall the providing mechanism consist of a multiplicity of specialist agencies, as the specialty boutique, or should it be built on the supermarket or department store model? The multipurpose center has significant appeal because it implies simplicity and directness; a one-door approach for numerous wants. This was the driving force behind the emergence of Charity Organization Societies in the nineteenth century. The complexities of industrial society doomed this one-door approach in the past. Can it be revived today?

It is too early to know whether we will succeed in bringing many services reasonably into a multipurpose, one-door type of operation rooted in neighborhood conditions, but there are signs of such movement. For the retarded and the aged, at least, there have evolved multipurpose agencies that undertake to provide a broad range of tangible and concrete services, as well as supportive counselling and assessment, under a single management which plans and directs the allocation of resources. For these populations the consumer wants are sufficiently clear, focused, and tangible to permit such an evolution. Some geriatric centers offer private apartment housing, sheltered institutional care, medical and nursing attention at home and in a medical-like institution, food service, psychological help, employment, recreation, adult education, and socialization all under one management. Certain community living centers for the retarded have similarly organized multiple services through one administration.

In the field of mental health and health care, generally, the evolution is less clear. Although hospitals are somewhat complex and comprehensive, their work usually stops at the hospital door. As for health-related social services, it is instructive to be reminded how much professions in the same field differ in their perceptions of each other, for this reinforces our awareness of the probable gap between consumer and provider perceptions. A series of studies (Twoomey, Briggs, and others) have observed that physicians and nurses expect social workers to handle practical matters such as arranging accommodation or physical care on discharge from hospital, to look after housing and financial needs, and to smooth out family relationships; whereas social workers in the same settings see their role much more clinically defined, that is, helping patients to use medical services given by others and helping them adjust to the realities of their physical condition.

Hospital social services, as for example, in the Veterans Administration, have moved to correct this contradiction. They have taken over responsibility for managing some home care and halfway house programs for early discharged hospital patients; they have supplemented information, counseling, and advisory functions with responsibility for mobilizing housing, financial, homemaker, and nursing home on behalf of the hospital's special clientele; and they often manage the linkage between hospital and community services to maintain some coherent continuity in treatment. It may be that the mismatch between provider and user perceptions will have to be resolved in some such fashion, and will be speeded up by the marketplace approach of the consumer.

The experience found in such illustrations suggests that the multipurpose center approach cannot survive if it relies primarily upon information, counseling, and advocacy on the behalf of consumers against other service systems. For some portion of consumers this may suffice, as Perlman's data suggest, but an agency thus limited in its helpfulness cannot yet be called either comprehensive or multifaceted.

To really meet consumer wants more broadly, some variety or cluster of tangible and intangible helps that consumers want, and want sufficiently strongly to seek out, is necessary. This forces planners either to consolidate a variety of tangible services into one organization, or to procure new funds with which to provide some set of services, tangible or intangible in nature, which are not yet around but that are clearly wanted. To rely solely, or even primarily, upon referral to other agencies, to coordinate service as casemanagers when there is no control over what is being coordinated, to pressure other agencies to favor your clients against others hardly provides the solid foundation with which to approach a consumer-oriented system.

Two approaches of a more general nature than that represented by agencies for the aging or retarded are now being tested. One involves an extension or improvement on the boutique or specialty approach. Many specialties are at least brought under one roof, but the specialty agencies also agree that the center administration will acquire and administer certain additional resources to provide some tangible services that none of the others are prepared to carry alone. Examples exist whereby transportation to agencies, day care for children, and the like are centrally administered.

An alternative approach involves the merger—not coordination—of numerous service providers mainly under the impetus of state government reorganization. Although this has moved very slowly, a few county examples of consolidation of public agencies exist and the weight of large-scale governmental reorganization will continue to operate against the current fragmentation.

The choice among approaches with which to better match wants and provision is seriously impeded by the rigidities of resource allocation for the human services. Most agencies find that demand by clients vastly exceeds resources available. The tangible services that consumers seem to want most, although not exclusively, are especially costly. Agencies are forced to protect themselves by limiting their offerings to the things they can give within their resource constraints. Many nonprofit agencies thus end up giving advice, counsel, and information. To adopt any other course would bankrupt them quickly.

It is assumed that "some one else" will meet most of the tangible wants expressed by consumers—for jobs, for medical care, for household help, for housing, for income upgrading, and even for *long-term* emotional support for the buffeted or overwhelmed person. It is easier for the limited resource agency to keep financially afloat by giving information and counseling, helping to "sort out" or to assess socially distressful situations—but only so long as clients keep coming and someone is willing to pay for this limited function. If users are truly consumers, they will be in a position to size up whether this is what they want or not. The Perlman data suggest that some consumers will keep coming but most will stop quickly unless the multiple service center can really deliver what is sought after.

The acquisition of resources to deliver what consumers really want is further frustrated by the fact that the human service system does not wholly operate on the same incentive system as does the material goods market. Limited income users cannot buy some social necessities and providers are reluctant to offer their services only for those who can and are willing to pay. Thus, clients as consumers are not yet really free of provider perceptions concerning what should be provided. The flaws of the philanthropic approach are being changed by new ways to subsidize the consumer (i.e. vouchers) or the provider directly, to increase responsiveness to consumer wants through contract purchase of services. The results of these changes are not yet apparent.

Part of the provider system does function on an economic model. Nursing home, hospitals, health services, and housing generally function because enough people have an income and a willingness to pay to support a provider system. The quasiproprietary services are heavily subsidized by tax funds through various channels, to reduce the cost to the paying client and to cover some, but not all, of the nonpaying users. Abuses in this arrangement, shoddy care, inaccessibility to many who are in need and who want these items add up to flaws in the performance of the pure marketplace concept for the consumer.

In the end, it can only be concluded that dissatisfaction is making waves that have shaken the earlier patterns of social service delivery. Temporary islets of new delivery forms are emerging, but no firm new foundation has yet been laid. The challenge is to construct a logical framework that is flexible enough to serve these ends: to recognize clusters of consumer wants; to meet these wants more comprehensively than before; to link up consumer groups with closely related service packages that include tangible and concrete offerings desired by consumers.

Competing models to serve these have developed: (1) the multipurpose center with a general purpose backed up by a package of concrete offerings; (2) the boutique approach, which through new activities emerges in response to consumer demands when economic arrangements permit; and (3) multipurpose service systems built around diagnostic groups such as the aged or the retarded. This study of the interface between consumer and provider goes a long way toward clarifying how these models may evolve. The dynamic tension that produces change is clearly articulated; it even helps us anticipate the direction of change in the future.

Robert Morris
Brandeis University
Waltham, Massachusetts

Preface

The interactions between an institution and the people who make use of it can be subtle, masked, and subject to differing interpretations. It is difficult to understand these encounters without examining them directly and unequivocally from the perspectives of both the users and the institution.

The study of social welfare institutions and their consumers, until quite recently, has been lopsided; it has been conducted primarily from the viewpoint of the providers of services. Issues in the organization and delivery of social services were considered to be difficulties that social agencies have with their clients. The distinction between "client" and "consumer" reveals an important change in viewpoint. "Client," in its origin and current usage, connotes dependency on the provider. "Consumer" refers to a person who acquires and uses goods and services to satisfy his needs.*

The consumer's perspective has emerged in the past ten years in all aspects of life in the United States with greater force and clarity than ever before. In social welfare, consumers' interests are being articulated and their influence mobilized partly as a response to inequities affecting the poor, racial and ethnic minorities, the old, and the rejected. In part the new voice of the consumer comes out of the discontent of people of all social classes as they confront large social agencies whose policies and practices are determined at remote distances.

This book provides a clearer picture of how and why consumers and providers of social services behave the way they do toward each other. In particular, my purpose is to examine the consumer perspective. This perspective recasts old problems into new forms; it helps us to see, for example, the troubles consumers have in benefitting from what providers offer.

The book is intended for practitioners and administrators and for students who are preparing to enter the human services or the social welfare field.

These questions are discussed: How do consumers present their problems to social agencies, and what kind of help do they expect? Are there "costs" that consumers pay even when services are free of charge? What is the similarity between consumer expectations and the things that social welfare agencies actually deliver? How do consumers differ among themselves, and are there

---

*It is interesting that Wilensky and Lebeaux, in their study of social welfare in the United States, employ "client" consistently in connection with the use of social services and "consumer" exclusively to refer to the buying of refrigerators, cars, and other goods and services in the commercial market. See Harold L. Wilensky and Charles N. Lebeaux, *Industrial Society and Social Welfare*, The Free Press, New York, 1965.

distinct types? How do social service organizations respond when confronted with consumer demands that exceed their capacities? Where can consumer advocates effectively function in the social services? And, finally, what are the implications of our findings for the planning and organization of services?

Consumers' interests in these issues ought to be better understood for reasons of equity and justice, because it is the consumer whose well-being is at stake. It is also important for practical reasons, because programs planned in consonance with the expectations and behavior of consumers are more likely to be used and, possibly, more apt to be effective.

The book is organized around the questions posed above and brings to bear on them an analysis of some recent experience in the delivery of social services. The case materials come from the neighborhood service centers that were established principally in the ghettoes of our cities during the last ten years. I draw in some detail on the experience of the Roxbury Multi-Service Center in Boston.

The fact that this book is about the personal social services—as distinguished, for example, from the social insurances and government aid for housing for the poor—does not imply that the services described in these pages are *per se* answers to massive problems of poverty, deprivation, and discrimination. In my opinion, the resolution of those problems will require far-reaching changes in the distribution of income and in the means of access to jobs, to quality health and education services, to housing, and to other goods and services.

But even if those goals were accepted and the requisite programs undertaken today, there will continue for some time to be a need for the services considered in this book. As a result of sickness, old age, and the cumulative damage produced by existing social conditions, some people will require help to achieve a level and quality of life acceptable to society and to themselves. Such help can be called palliative and, if seen from a sufficient distance, trivial.

Many other prople, regardless of income or age, will continue to need personal social services to deal with the normal demands of living in a complex society.

For all people who need their assistance the personal social services can sometimes ease pain and help people become more capable of acting, individually and collectively, in their own behalf. Those purposes are worthy of being pursued; the means of realizing them warrant our attention.

Robert Perlman

Acknowledgements

Many people have helped to shape this book.*

Wyatt C. Jones directed the collection and processing of the data from the Roxbury Multi-Service Center. I am grateful to him for reducing those voluminous records to manageable form and for his help in the first stages of analyzing the data. Action for Boston Community Development cooperated in giving permission to use the case records which they had received from the Center.

I am indebted to John Douds and Phyllis Silverman for ideas which contributed much to the typology of consumers that are presented in these pages.

The case material gathered in the course of Dr. Silverman's research proved to be particularly useful in illustrating the consumer typology.

I am in debt to Brian Wharf for permission to use his study of the relationship of the Roxbury Center to other agencies in the community.

Gertrude Cuthbert, the first Executive Director of the Roxbury Multi-Service Center, and Hubert Jones, who succeeded her, were generous of their time and assistance in this project. Regina Keating was particularly helpful with the case records. Frances Gelber and Nancy Robinson provided useful reactions from the point of view of the RMSC staff.

I want to express my appreciation for the comments on earlier drafts of this material received from Arnold Gurin, Wyatt Jones, Lorraine Klerman, Robert Morris, Bernice Perlman, Martin Rein, and Jack Rothman.

Mary Hyde was painstaking and patient in handling the computer program. I am grateful to Ruth Daniels for her care and interest in preparing several drafts of this work. And I want to thank Judy Perlman and Richard Daniels for devoting many patient hours to the statistics and tables and to David Perlman for his proof-reading.

All these people contributed much to this study. Its final form remains my responsibility.

There is something else to be acknowledged. As program development director at Action for Boston Community Development, I had an active part in the planning of the center in Roxbury and shared with others in the hopes for what

*The study was supported by Grant No. 390-C2 from the Office of Research and Demonstrations, Social and Rehabilitative Service, Department of Health, Education, and Welfare.

it would achieve. Without relinquishing interest or pride in its accomplishments, I have tried in these pages to find in its experience some lessons from which we can all learn.

R.P.

Contents

Tables

Illustrations

1

Consumer-Oriented Service Centers

It is important and timely to give attention to the behavior of social service consumers and providers toward each other. We are at one of those junctures when critical issues in the development and delivery of social services are being decided. The current debate goes to the very purposes of our vast machinery of social welfare. At issue are the nature of the programs, the criteria for evaluating them, and the ways in which they should be controlled and planned.

To stress the consumer's perspective does not mean that his is the only one that has a bearing on these issues. Other forces and constraints must also be taken into account. But the consumer's side has been neglected and that fact is relevant to several important developments that are now under way.

One of these is the removal of large numbers of people from institutions for the mentally ill, the retarded, the aged, and those convicted of legal offenses. This places a strain on our meager knowledge of how consumers make use of social services on a voluntary basis. The virtual emptying of many institutions is being done with the expectation that their former residents can make satisfactory adjustments because they will have the support of social services in the community. Whether or how such services will be used becomes then a significant element in de-institutionalization.

Another development is the separation of services from income maintenance programs and the interest in creating a general service delivery system not addressed exclusively to public welfare recipients. This is part of a broader movement whose stated goal is to produce a more coherent and effective structure in the human services. The reorganization of health, welfare, and correctional agencies in a number of states is gaining momentum. In this context, our knowledge of reciprocal behaviors between consumer and agency is woefully inadequate.

What we do know about consumer patterns has been augmented by the study and experimentation of the past ten years. It is important, however, to appreciate the limitations of the research that has been done, since our understandings are colored by the questions researchers have asked and by the sources of information from which they derived their answers. The research to date has been heavily concentrated in the health services, including psychiatry, and social casework. As a result we know much less about a large range of services and problems that lie outside those boundaries.

It seems wisest at this point to be cowardly about defining the social services, and to defer that prickly issue to Chapter 9.[1] In general we shall be considering services delivered to individuals, families, and groups that are addressed to developmental, rehabilitative, supportive, and preventive purposes. The personal social services do not include education, health, housing, and income maintenance programs, but do include arranging for access, advocacy, and protection in those systems.

In a review of research on health and welfare services, McKinlay included only a few references to the personal social services, and these concerned mainly social casework, a type of service and method that has had a strong impact on the broader field of nonmedical services.[2] This is understandable since casework, until recently, furnished one of the few models, other than the health services, for recipient provider interactions. The conceptualization of casework as an essentially psychotherapeutic process has directed much of the research toward the client-worker relationship, the techniques of helping, and the personal characteristics of the helper and the helped, to the neglect of other factors.

The studies that have been done demonstrate a marked tendency to ask (implicitly if not explicitly) whether the consumers are performing appropriately in the roles required by agency policies and procedures. Researchers have studied whether consumers' attitudes toward a service are conducive to making the best use of what is offered and whether, for example, clients are willing to maintain contact for as often and as long as the agency deems necessary.

In comparison with this concern for the client-worker relationship, proportionately less attention has been given to the programs and resources of social agencies and how they are perceived by consumers, especially by people who think of their problems as environmental and material rather than interpersonal and emotional.

If we take the agency service as the given, and then study the consumer's response to it, we run the risk of missing important aspects of the consumer's purposes and preferences. The result may be to bury some of the very factors that make for dissonance between user and service. Furthermore, considering the uncertainties that surround the effectiveness of many social services, it is risky to assume that there must be a close fit between the service as offered and the consumer's capacity or inclination to use it as prescribed.

A policy of responding to consumer demands sidesteps some difficult issues

[1] For an extensive discussion of these issue, see Alfred J. Kahn, *Social Policy and Social Services*, New York, Random House, 1973.

[2] John B. McKinlay, "Some Approaches and Problems in the Study of the Use of Services—An Overview," *Journal of Health and Social Behavior*, published by the American Sociological Association, Vol. 13, No. 2, June, 1972, pp. 115—152.

concerning the effectiveness of services once they have been delivered. How do we know that what the client asks for will, in the end, be the most useful thing that could have been done for him? Or that, at least, it will be better than following the professional's judgment? The answer, of course, is that we do not know.

In general, effectiveness in the personal social services is problematic.[3] This difficulty extends to the very definition of their purposes—a matter that we examine in the final chapter—and reflects an inability to come to terms with the meaning of performance. Rein writes:

> The units of activity to be performed cannot be specified nor made comparable among different programs. This makes it difficult to study the more important relationship between performance standards and behavior outcomes. The failure to standardize services makes efforts to evaluate their effectiveness indeterminate, since countercriticism absorbs the imputed failure and attributes it to the low quality of the inputs.[4]

Research on the outcome of what might be called "consumer's choice" is extremely limited. The valuable study by Mayer and Timms to which we shall refer surveyed clients' satisfactions and dissatisfactions among English working-class people as a result of their contacts with caseworkers. However, important as their study is for exploring "the clash of perspectives" between clients and caseworkers, it did not set out to study the effects of following clients' preferences as to the nature of the service to be rendered.

This inquiry does not attempt to deal directly with effectiveness, except for its concern with the circumstances in which the service had no possibility of affecting the outcome—that is, when an agency takes no action on the problems presented to it.

A lack of effectiveness was only one of the strong criticisms that were being made of the social services in the 1960's. The services, it was charged, were inaccessible to people who needed them most; they were especially inappropriate for the poor and the minority groups; and they were ill coordinated and lacking in comprehensiveness.

Largely in response to these criticisms, hundreds of neighborhood service centers sprang up in the ghettoes.[5] A national survey identified 2518 centers in

---

[3] Joel Fischer, "Is Casework Effective? A Review," *Social Work*, Journal of the National Association of Social Workers, Vol. 18, No. 1, January 1973; Scott Briar and Henry Miller, *Problems and Issues in Social Casework*, New York: Columbia University Press, 1971, p. 165.

[4] Martin Rein, "Decentralization and Citizen Participation in Social Services," *Public Administration Review*, Vol. XXXII, October 1972, p. 687.

[5] Some centers were planned and operated by community action agencies with funding from the Office of Economic Opportunity and later from HEW and other sources. Others are being supported under new concepts of community mental health; some are funded by churches or other local groups.

1970.[6] In the minds of their planners, the centers were to be everything the traditional agencies were not. Above all, they were to orient themselves to the patterns and preferences of consumers.

The new organizations were designed to fulfill three main functions. They served as *access points* to health and welfare services and to parts of the commercial market by offering information, advice, referral and brokerage. They were *pressure points*, seeking to alter the policies and practices of other organizations. This was done for the individual through advocacy of his claims and for groups or populations (welfare clients, tenants, and others) through collective and community actions. Third, the centers offered *direct services* where they were inadequate or lacking. They included, for instance, legal aid, employment assistance, day care for children, recreation, counseling, and home help.

Walz describes the distinguishing features of the neighborhood centers as follows.

1. *A separate agency for the poor.* To counter strong resentments against established social welfare agencies and their middle- and upper-income decision-makers, the center was to be a separate agency "at least symbolically owned by the poor."

2. *Aggressive out-reach.* The centers were to reach people who lacked information about available services or the will to take the initiative to obtain them. They also were to demonstrate the inadequacy of existing services and this would be a first step toward social action and change.

3. *Convenience factor.* The centers were placed in accessible locations, to bring services into the street and home, and the working hours of the center staff were adjusted to the needs of the residents.

4. *De-bureaucratization* or humanization of service delivery involves the removal of symbols of formality, such as paperwork, and changing the antiseptic climate of agencies. Conversely, it meant "workers in rolled-up sleeves," "lots of black and minority faces," open waiting rooms, and convenient coffeepots.

5. *Instant service.* In order to avoid long delays and endless referrals, especially for people who often require help at the moment, services were to be provided immediately upon request.

6. *Consumer control* called for policy making and advisory boards extensively composed of low-income people.

7. *Militancy* would entail the use of conflict and direct action techniques to change the status quo.

---

[6] Edward J. O'Donnell and Otto M. Reid, "The Multi-Service Neighborhood Center: Preliminary Findings from a National Survey," *Welfare in Review*, May–June 1971, Vol. 9, No. 3, pp. 1–8.

8. *Use of the indigenous nonprofessional.* Both scarcity and distrust of professionally trained workers stimulated the use of low-income residents as paid helpers in the centers. This was to be a means of improving communication with consumers as well as a way of providing dignified work and increased incomes to some of the poor.

9. *Popularization of new services and service methods.* Although not new, such programs as legal aid and client advocacy would become better publicized and more widely used through the neighborhood service centers.

10. *Concept of comprehensive care.* The centers were to deal with a broader range of problems than many other agencies and were to offer a larger spectrum of services as an antidote to fragmentation.[7]

Generally, Americans try to cope with their problems on their own or with the help of relatives, friends, and neighbors. When these efforts fail, they turn to formal organizations.[8] From one perspective, the neighborhood service centers are part of the professionalized service system. But they also serve as bridges between the kin and friendship network and the organized services. In the latter sense they can be considered mechanisms for helping people, especially the poor, to find or more accurately wrest benefits from the marketplace (employers, landlords, and retail merchants) and from the social services broadly defined (public welfare, public housing, schools, health facilities, and the courts, for example).

The political machine and the settlement house at the turn of the century performed these same mediating functions. Witness one of Boston's politicians:

> I think there has got to be in every ward a guy that any bloke can go to when he's in trouble and get help—not justice and the law, but help, no matter what he's done.
>
> Is somebody out of a job? We do our best to place him, and not necessarily on the public payroll. Does the family run into arrears with the landlord or butcher? We lend a helping hand. Do the kids need shoes or clothing, or the mother a doctor? We do what we can. . . .[9]

A prime assumption underlying the establishment of the neighborhood service centers was that they could reach and help the unserved by being more *accessible* in terms of their location, their open atmosphere, and their style of

[7] Thomas H. Walz, "The Emergence of the Neighborhood Service Center," *Public Welfare*, Vol. 27, No. 2, April 1969, pp. 147–156.

[8] David Landy, "Problems of the Person Seeking Help," in Meyer N. Zald, ed., *Social Welfare Institutions*, John Wiley & Sons, 1965, p. 569; Eliot Friedson, "Client Control and Medical Practice," *American Journal of Sociology*, LXV (1960), pp. 376–77.

[9] Martin "Mahatma" Lomasney, c. 1900, quoted in Ralph G. Martin, *The Bosses*, New York: G. P. Putnam's Sons, 1964, pp. 16–17.

intake and operation. This stemmed from the hope that the centers could find remedies for the deficiencies attributed to the established agencies.[10]

It was charged that certain services were not available where people lived and experienced most of their problems. Some services were located too far away for people who lacked the carfare or the energy to get "downtown." Other services were available in the neighborhood but people did not know of their existence. Still others were made inaccessible by red tape, limited hours, waiting lists, and impersonal regulations that were baffling to people who did not know how to negotiate their way through large bureaucracies.

There were charges that rigid rules and insulting behavior by some of the agency personnel stripped people of their dignity. Many services carried a stigma dating back to the repressive features of the Elizabethan poor laws.

It was argued that the antidote to these conditions lay in offering a neighborhood-based service that anyone could enter easily with any question or problem and that would respond with interest, warmth, alacrity, and respect. One aspect of a welcoming climate that would make the centers more psychologically accessible was the racial character of its personnel. Although the Center in Roxbury, for instance, had a few white people on its staff, its Board of Directors and staff were predominantly black. It was anticipated that black people would use the facility more than whites in proportion to their numbers in the surrounding community.

Most of the centers had important functions beyond those concerned with the delivery of services. They organized neighborhood residents for social action and community development, and these became the primary activities in some places. We do not attempt to review this experience with neighborhood organization. Two other aspects of the centers are beyond the scope of this study. One concerns the specialized centers that offered only one service (for example, legal aid or job training) or services to one group, such as the aged. Another aspect deals with the employment and training of paraprofessionals and the development of new career opportunities for poor people in the human services.

Our primary interest is in the interface between consumer and service. Because

[10] This discussion draws on the following: Thomas H. Walz, op. cit.; Edward J. O'Donnell and Marilyn M. Sullivan, "Service Delivery and Social Action Through the Neighborhood Center: A Review of Research," Vol. 7, No. 6, *Welfare in Review*, Nov.–Dec. 1969; Alfred J. Kahn, *Studies in Social Policy and Planning*, New York: Russell Sage Foundation, 1969, pp. 245 and ff.; Harold R. Johnson, "Neighborhood Services," in *Encyclopedia of Social Work*, New York: National Association of Social Workers, 16th Issue, 1971, Vol. I, pp. 865–872; Harry C. Bredemeier, "The Socially Handicapped and the Agencies," *Mental Health of the Poor*, Frank Reissman, Jerome Cohen, Arthur Pearl, eds., New York: The Free Press of Glencoe, 1964, pp. 109–119; Hettie Jones, "Neighborhood Service Centers," in H. H. Weissman, ed., *Individual and Group Services in the Mobilization for Youth Experience*, New York: Association Press, 1967, pp. 33–53.

the neighborhood centers set out to address problems involved in that interaction, their experience is relevant. More is known about them now than in the euphoric days when Walz described them and when Miller and Reissman wrote that the centers "had the potential of increasing and fusing the supply of services" . . . and encouraging "the maximum use of services through coordination, reduction of red tape, greater communication, liaison, and so on."[11] Or when Kahn wrote that the investment in these programs seemed to have "purchased relatively little direct personal service or even accountability . . . the sum total of information, diagnostic service, counseling, placements, day care, recreation, or homemaking produced was quite modest."[12]

Again, our purpose in examining the neighborhood centers is not to evaluate their performance but to draw on their experience so that some insight is gained about the questions of general interest concerning consumers and social services.[13] The centers lend themselves to this purpose. They serve the poor, which is the responsibility of a large part of this country's social services, and they invite people to come with any problem and, for this reason, offer a wider canvas of consumer behavior than agencies with more narrowly defined functions and clientele. Their experience highlights the demands that go unsatisfied by the social welfare establishment and the commercial market.

Our information is drawn primarily from the Roxbury Multi-Service Center (RMSC) in Boston's black community. In addition, we draw from reports on other neighborhood centers, principally those under the aegis of Lincoln Hospital in the Bronx and Mobilization for Youth on the Lower East Side of New York City.[14] In many respects, the center in Roxbury is typical of the 2500 that were operating in 1970.

[11] S. M. Miller and Frank Reissman, *Social Class and Social Policy*, New York: Basic Books, 1968, p. 247.

[12] Kahn, *op. cit.,* p. 42.

[13] For evaluations of multiservice centers see Robert Perlman and David Jones, *Neighborhood Service Centers*, Washington, D.C.; U.S. Department of Health, Education, and Welfare, Office of Juvenile Delinquency and Youth Development, 1967; Kirschner Associates, "A Description and Evaluation of Neighborhood Centers, A Report for the Office of Economic Opportunity", Albuquerque, N.M., 1966, mimeographed; Bertram M. Beck et al., "Neighborhood Service Centers: A Study and Recommendations," in *Examination of the War on Poverty (Senate)*, Staff and Consultant Reports, III, 733–786; O'Donnell and Sullivan, op. cit., Alfred J. Kahn, op. cit., pp. 40–44 and Ch. VII; Melvin B. Mogulof, "Neighborhood Service Centers," *Encyclopedia of Social Work*, op. cit., pp. 857–864; Abt Associates Inc., "A Study of the Neighborhood Center Pilot Program," Vol. 1, prepared for the Executive Office of the President, Bureau of the Budget, 1969.

[14] See Stanley Lehmann, "Selected Self-Help: A Study of Clients of a Community Social Psychiatry Service," *American Journal of Psychiatry, 126*:10, April 1970, pp. 1444–1454; and Hettie Jones, *op. cit.*

The RMSC was established by a city-wide agency, Action for Boston Community Development (ABCD), and was planned and operated with support from the Ford Foundation's "gray areas program," President Kennedy's antidelinquency program, and later President Johnson's "war on poverty."[15]

In its formative months, ABCD commissioned experts to study social problems in Boston and write position papers to guide the new organization. Whitney M. Young, Jr. was asked in 1961 to conduct a study of Roxbury-North Dorchester, an area of 80,000 people that had absorbed successive waves of Irish and Jewish immigrants and, since 1935, Negroes. Young found that this was:

> primarily a residential area, with practically equal numbers of Negro and white residents. Within its boundaries, however, there is a tendency for neighborhoods to be predominantly Negro or predominantly white. . . .
>
> Many of the neighborhoods have unsound housing that is overcrowded. Poor health is a factor in these same neighborhoods and both poor housing and poor health are found where there is a high proportion of Negroes. . . . this part of Boston ranks high in crime, delinquency, broken homes, illegitimacy, dependence on public assistance and unemployment. Roxbury-North Dorchester, in short, is a district with severe social problems.[16]

At that time the area was in the throes of an urban renewal project. Between 1960 and 1970, Roxbury lost one-fourth of its people and its housing; its population changed from 44 percent black to 67 percent.[17]

Young's report, based on four neighborhood meetings and interviews with community leaders, painted a picture of neglect and inadequacy in services. He found them unevenly distributed; the neighborhoods with the greatest population densities and the highest rates of social problems had fewer facilities.

Residents were sharply critical in their comments about medical, mental health, and dental services, about education, employment, recreation, and family and child welfare, and about legal aid and protective services. For example, they said that employment agencies were not forceful in promoting jobs for residents of Roxbury. Mental health and family services were inadequate and people were not informed about those that did exist. The schools had insufficient services to

---

[15] See Stephan Thernstrom, *Poverty, Planning and Politics in the New Boston: The Origins of ABCD*, New York: Basic Books, Inc., 1969, and Peter Marris and Martin Rein, *Dilemmas of Social Reform*, New York: Atherton Press, 1967. ABCD also developed the John F. Kennedy Center in Charlestown, a predominantly Irish-American working class section of Boston.

[16] Whitney M. Young, Jr., *A Preliminary Exploration of Social Conditions and Needs in the Roxbury-North Dorchester GNRP* (mimeographed), Boston: Action for Boston Community Development, June 1961, p. 12.

[17] *News from United Community Services*, Boston: United Community Services (mimeographed), August 2, 1971. North Dorchester changed from 10 percent black to 34 percent in the 1960's.

give individualized attention to students, and this was associated with high drop-out rates.

Other surveys conducted by ABCD in 1963–1964 confirmed the view that the services for a population of 80,000, many of whom were poor and 6,000 of whom were public welfare recipients, were meager and maldistributed.[18] The Department of Public Welfare, the Department of Public Health, and the Visiting Nurse Association each maintained three offices in the area. There were five settlement houses and two church-sponsored community centers.

Four voluntary family agencies served some 900 families.[19] A child guidance center for preschool children was located in the area but only 15 percent of those in the treatment program were from Roxbury-North Dorchester. Only a few day care centers were in operation in a district with a large proportion of working mothers. The surveys listed more than a dozen city-wide and statewide agencies which were not located in the area but provided services there, but interviews with clergymen and with the staffs of group service agencies emphasized gaps in health and welfare services.

In short, although some services were available, the general opinion at the time of Young's study was that Roxbury-North Dorchester was grossly underserved by social welfare agencies. Young made a number of recommendations looking toward the creation of a viable interracial community and urged that genuine responsibility be given to organizations within Roxbury to develop and implement a social plan for the community. One of the final recommendations, stemming from the dramatic evidence that citizens and social service agencies were missing each other, was a call for more communication, but "beyond this it is crucial to establish a community-centered facility with limited emergency services but unlimited referral possibilities."

Well before Young's study Boston's welfare council (United Community Services) had recommended the organization of "community social services centers". Two years after his report was issued, the city's Redevelopment Authority, overwhelmed by the problems of relocating people displaced by urban renewal, was promoting the establishment of a multiservice center to offer

---

[18] The area covered by these surveys was the General Neighborhood Renewal Plan (GNRP) district of Roxbury-North Dorchester, with a population of 82,247 or 23,000 families in 1960.

As of June 1964 the Department of Public Welfare reported these caseloads: AFDC, 2577; OAA, 1589; Disability, 408; Medical Aid to the Aged, 370; General Relief, 248. During 1963 the Division of Child Guardianship served 565, 145 of whom were taken into care. (Unpublished report, ABCD.)

[19] These included the nonsectarian family agency with 541 cases, the American Red Cross with 301, and the Jewish and Catholic family service agencies with a total of 66 cases. Others such as Big Brothers, Legal Aid, and missionary societies, served smaller numbers of residents.

instant diagnosis and specialists to follow through with relocatees' problems. The Authority hoped that this would at least remove obstacles to the renewal effort and at best match social rehabilitation with physical renewal of the community. Influences on the planning of the RMSC, coupled with financial support, flowed from both the Redevelopment Authority and the welfare council.[20] The planning of the center stretched over many months, mainly because it involved efforts to obtain commitments of staff or funds from a number of agencies.

The plan called for a center to be organized around three main service units: employment, legal aid, and a general social service. A staff of neighborhood workers was to be concerned with community organization, housing problems, and case-finding. It took a few months before the core staff, excluding those on loan, reached the level of 25, where it remained for most of the period under review in this study. The RMSC had a board of directors of 15 Roxbury residents and 4 people representing city-wide organizations. This community-based board was a departure from the pattern Whitney Young had found.

The RMSC can be considered typical in many respects of the neighborhood centers studied in the national survey by O'Donnell and Reid, although it was larger than most of them in the number of people served and the size of the staff and budget. It provided the same services that most centers offered.[21] It differed in that it had as a part of its operation professionals from other agencies. These included several caseworkers from Boston's family service

[20] Edward Newman, *A Case Study of Social Planning Opportunities and Limitations*, (Unpublished doctoral dissertation, Brandeis University, 1968).

[21] The percentages below represent the proportion of neighborhood centers which offered the services listed. The asterisks denote services provided by the Roxbury center. The information is from the report by O'Donnell and Reid, *op. cit.*

Type of Service	Percentage of Centers Providing Service
*Counselling	82
Educational programs	74
*Recreation	69
*Employment	57
*Health	43
*Elderly	39
*Welfare liaison	39
*Housing	35
Consumer	31
*Child welfare	29
*Legal aid	26
Determining Medicaid elegibility	22
Determining public assistance eligibility	18
Vocational rehabilitation	16

*Service offered by RMSC 1965—67.

agency; two lawyers from the Boston Legal Aid Society, who functioned however quite independently of the Center; and a psychiatrist on a part-time basis from the mental health program administered by Boston University's medical school.

A representative of the Welfare Department was assigned to the Center but was withdrawn after a few months. For almost a year the Visiting Nurse Association had a nurse at the Center primarily to help the staff identify health problems and resources. When she left, the staff was expected to continue this concern for health needs. In the fall of 1965 a Home Development unit was established in Social Service to work with families in their homes. This unit operated for a year and a half and was then discontinued.

The substantial autonomy maintained by the branch office of the Boston Legal Aid Society which was located within the Center requires additional comment. The Society's interpretation of confidentiality between lawyer and client resulted in a decision not to participate in the central record system at RMSC. Hence *some* information is missing on the clients who were referred to the Legal Aid service, although more data are available on those who were served jointly by the lawyers and other staff members at the Center.

By no means, however, do all of the deficiencies in the data in this study result from the fact that the Legal Aid Society did not provide information for the central file. For example, while the race, sex and age were recorded on 92 percent of the RMSC users, marital status, education, and household composition are known for only 60 percent. A reading of the records suggests strongly that much which was in fact said and done went unrecorded. In many cases, for instance, there is no indication that the client broke off contact and there seems to have been every intention on the part of both client and worker to take some further steps. Doubtless some of these intentions were not fulfilled, but it is reasonable to suppose that some were and that these records are simply incomplete, though on the whole large amounts of information were carefully recorded.

Two extremes in recording are represented by the Employment Service and Social Service. The former had what appear to be many incomplete records and the latter full and detailed recording. This reflects the training and practice of social workers who place considerable emphasis on such recording. These limitations in the data compel us to be cautious in making generalizations. It is advisable to put less stress on the cases for which we have meager information and more on those for which we have more adequate data.

The recording system, part of the Program Design which had been developed by a planning staff over a period of many months, provided for "the rapid and flexible flow of information" through a centralized file. Each record was to include a Registration Form, a Face Sheet, an Assessment Form, and an entry for every contact with the client. These records were to be available to all workers in contact with the client.

Another device designed to achieve integration of services was the designation of an "anchor worker" for those people who "cannot maintain a relationship with a number of different workers at the same time." The anchor worker would either provide all services to these clients or would arrange for them with other members of the RMSC staff. Wherever possible, services would be channeled through the anchor worker.

The Program Design announced the goals of the Center in these words:

> The multiservice center will concentrate its efforts on families facing serious problems with respect to employment, physical and mental health, involvement with the courts, child-rearing, home-management, and other environmental and personal difficulties. The program is designed to reach out to families and individuals who have the greatest needs but are the least willing or able to seek out and use help. The center will:
>
> 1. Provide health, welfare and related services that are visible and accessible on a neighborhood and district level.
>
> 2. Develop effective techniques of providing health and welfare services to reach families and individuals who do not respond to the present system of services.
>
> 3. Make available a battery of services coordinated around the family as a unit to insure long-term effectiveness.[22]

Two days after Christmas in 1964 in a renovated apartment house on a main street in Roxbury, the executive director and a few staff members swept the floor, set up some card tables, and opened the door for the first people who came in looking for help. This study draws on the Center's experiences with the 4061 people who were registered as clients through March, 1967—and more importantly on their experiences with the Center.

[22] Action for Boston Community Development, Inc. and United Community Services of Metropolitan Boston, *Program Design for the Roxbury Multi-Service Center*, Revised, June 10, 1964.

2
The Problem
Is in the Eye of the Beholder

For the purposes of our discussion it is useful to distinguish between people's "conditions" and their "problems." Conditions are those human circumstances that are quite real and palpable, such as being unemployed or widowed, but that remain to be defined as problems. Problems are those situations that people bring to a social service agency because they want help.

Many conditions are closely associated with people's status and characteristics—their age, race, sex, income, roles. Vulnerability to loss of job, certain health conditions, and discrimination are examples of conditions that do not fall randomly in the total population but are highly correlated with one's socioeconomic circumstances.

But whether someone has a "problem" with a child, a job, or a landlord is a matter of judgment. Problems do not have an objective, unambiguous meaning. How people and agencies define them therefore has important implications. On one side the consumers' definitions will influence when and where they go for assistance—indeed whether they go at all—what their expectations will be and how much time and effort they want to invest in getting help.

On the other side, the policies of social agencies rest on their definitions of problems and this is reflected in the kind of services they offer, to whom they offer them, and what methods they employ. In other words, the agency's concept of the consumer's problem shapes what the agency believes the latter needs.

These considerations raise some critical questions. How do people present their problems and how do their problems correspond to their socioeconomic characteristics, especially race, sex, and role. What cultural and ideological factors underlie the manner in which problems are defined for purposes of taking action on them? Whose definition prevails: the consumer's or the social agency's?

The experience of the Roxbury Center can be instructive in exploring these issues for, like the other neighborhood centers, it was dedicated to openness and receptivity to the consumer's definition of his predicament. The RMSC intake procedure was designed to capture as accurately as possible the consumer's perception of his situation.

13

The program design stated that "the Receptionist will first ask the client how the Center can be of help and will then listen to the client describe the problem for which he is seeking help." The Receptionist was to record the client's response *verbatim* and was then to determine to which service to assign him—Legal, Employment, or the general Social Services. The first worker in a service unit[1] who saw the client was to repeat the question the Receptionist had asked, that is, "How the Center could be of help?" and the second statement of the problem was to be recorded.[2]

It must be noted that the recording of people's problems inevitably involves judgments on the part of workers and some transposition of this material into prescriptive terms. A reading of the verbatim statements, which appear in the Appendix, makes it clear that while the instruction was to write down the words of the client, some of the formulations shade over into assessments of what he "needs." This is obvious, for example, in the difference between the statements "Wants to find a job" and "Needs employment counseling."

The receptionists referred people to the three services in almost identical numbers during the first two years of the Center's existence.[3] They sent to the Employment Service requests for jobs, training, and further schooling, for the most part. Legal Aid was called upon to handle desertion, divorce, and separation; legal questions involving children; and cases concerning landlords, employers, and retail merchants. Social Service handled a varied range of problems mostly revolving around family difficulties, housing, financial need, health, and complaints about schools. Almost half of the health problems were identified as mental health problems and referred to Social Service. In the

---

[1] It would be interesting to know how much time was devoted to the initial intake interview with the service workers. That information is available for only 43 percent of the clients. Of these, 24.5 percent of the interviews took up to one-half hour; 60.2 percent ran from 30 to 60 minutes and 15.1 percent exceeded one hour.

[2] A code of 300 items was developed from the verbatim statements and was consolidated into 31 problem types and then further into eight main problem areas. The frequency distribution for the main verbatim statements is given in the Appendix.

[3] The receptionists sent 1224 clients to Employment, 1225 to Social Service, and 1235 to Legal Aid. Instead of this remarkably even distribution of people, 36 percent of the problems were referred to Social Service, 29 percent to Employment, and 26 percent to Legal.

Some 200 particularly complex cases were referred to the Center's administrators. A visiting nurse was assigned to the Center in its first months of operation and 25 clients were sent to her. In addition there were a few cases on which there is no information. In all, 387 cases are classified in our analysis as other than Legal, Employment or Social Service. There were fewer than 100 simultaneous referrals by the receptionists to a second service.

Table 1

Race-Sex of RMSC Users[a]	Percent
Black women	61.8
Black men	26.0
White women	9.3
White men	2.9
Total	100.0

(*N* = 4061; 282 missing observations)

[a]Information on other characteristics is available for 60 percent of the clients. Within this group, 39 percent were married; 27 percent were separated, widowed or divorced, and 27 percent had never been married. The median number in the household was 3.4 and the number of children 1.4. One-fourth of the clients for whom we have data had no formal education; 14 percent had completed elementary school and 59 percent had more than nine years of schooling. Birthplace is known for half the clients and of these, half were born in the South and 35 percent in the Greater Boston area.

absence of health personnel, problems of physical health were also referred to Social Service. About 200 housing problems were referred to the Neighborhood Workers.

Who were the people who brought these problems? And who presented which problems? Nine out of ten were black. Sixty percent were black women. The people were rather evenly distributed in age between 15 and 54 years, with few over 55 (see Tables 1 and 2). The typical consumer was a black woman 35 years old with one or two children.

Table 2
Ages of RMSC Users[a]

Age	Percent Female	Percent Male	Percent Total
14–24	29.8	34.9	31.2
25–34	33.0	27.5	31.5
35–54	31.5	30.1	31.1
55–64	3.4	4.9	3.8
65 +	2.3	2.7	2.4
Total	100.0	100.1	100.0

(*N* = 4061; 317 missing observations)

[a]See the footnote to Table 1.

Table 3
RMSC Clients by Race, Sex, and Age as a Percentage
of the Population Over 14 Years of Age in the Catchment Area

Race-Sex	Clients as Percentage of Population Over 14 Years of Age
Black women	10.4
Black men	5.7
White women	5.4
White men	1.8
Age Group	
15—24	9.1
25—34	10.8
35—54	7.7
55 and over	2.4
All clients	8.2

[a]This covers the 50,000 people in the 11 census tracts in which 64 percent of the RMSC clients lived.

Most of the people who used the RMSC were participants in what Rainwater describes as "a lower class Negro community," created and maintained by two primary forces: economic marginality and racial oppression.[4] Our interest in this study, however, is not in the unique features of a black community *as* black, but in the orientations that consumers bring to their use of the social services.

Black women came to the Roxbury Center at twice the rate of either black men or white women and five times the rate of white men. And younger people came in larger proportions than older ones. Table 3 shows the percentages of each group over 14 years of age who became users of the RMSC. As to the heavy use by women, Lehmann found a similar phenomenon in the Bronx, where they constituted 76 percent of the clientele but only 63 percent of a sample of households.

The Roxbury and Bronx figures contrast sharply with what Walker found at the John F. Kennedy Center in Boston's Irish-American area, Charlestown, where only 42 percent of the clients were women. He concluded that the service seekers tend to be male in Charlestown and female in Roxbury, which "is consistent with the theory that, in the black community, women are more likely to be heads of households and, as a result, are more likely to be the family's

[4] Lee Rainwater, *Behind Ghetto Walls: Black Families in a Federal Slum,* Chicago: Aldine-Atherton, Inc., 1970, Chapter 13.

Table 4
Presenting Problems of RMSC Clients by Race-Sex
(N = 3779)

	Black Women	Black Men	White Women	White Men
Employment	18.3	42.2	10.7	21.3
Family	23.9	10.1	29.0	12.7
Financial	17.1	9.6	13.3	14.2
Housing	16.2	8.9	13.8	9.1
Legal	8.7	12.3	17.2	19.3
Health	6.6	5.2	9.1	14.2
Education and training	6.8	9.0	3.8	5.6
Information	2.3	2.7	3.0	3.6
	99.9	100.0	99.9	100.0

primary adult link with the institutions of the larger society such as the social welfare system, the school system, and the job market."[5]

The strong relationship between a person's problem and his demographic characteristics—especially the combination of race and sex—is evident in the Roxbury data. Table 4 is based on "presenting problems," that is, statements made either to the Receptionist or to the first service worker. There were no significant changes in the problem distributions beyond the point of intake.

Most striking, though certainly to be expected, is the extent to which black men came to the Center in connection with jobs. Some 42 percent of the black men's presenting problems concerned employment. Those under 25 years of age were looking especially for seasonal and part-time jobs and more training; those over 35 simply to find a job, or, in some instances, to locate a better job. One-third of the black men's presenting problems were evenly divided among legal, family, and financial concerns.

Black women, by contrast, brought a much higher proportion of family problems and financial and housing needs. One-fourth of their presenting problems related to family difficulties, but only one-fifth involved employment. By comparison with the black men, the women came twice as often in connection with problems affecting family life, finances, and housing and only half as often with respect to employment problems.

The profile of presenting problems was quite different for whites. Both white men and women brought more family problems than their black counterparts,

[5] Walter Lorenzo Walker, "The War on Poverty and the Poor: A Study of Race, Poverty and a Program," (unpublished doctoral dissertation, Brandeis University, 1970).

but only half as frequently did they present employment needs. The whites, both men and women, brought more legal and health problems.

The data leave little doubt that race and sex are significant in shaping the use of social services, for reasons that are all too apparent. Race or ethnicity and sex go far toward determining the character of a person's social and economic position and therefore what conditions he or she experiences.

Lehmann reported that while Puerto Rican clients at the Bronx neighborhood centers tended to have family and financial problems, the black client, who had been in the New York area a much longer time, was more concerned with employment and housing.[6]

Among black clients in Roxbury, sex made for noteworthy differences in the problems they brought to the RMSC. Given the unemployment situation among black men, jobs loomed much larger in the difficulties they presented. In the light of the considerable number of female-headed households, it is understandable why black women, relative to black men, showed twice as many family, financial and housing needs at the RMSC. Some of the white clients were older Jewish people, who encountered troubles with their health and with their landlords; they brought proportionately more health and legal problems to the RMSC than blacks did.

These variations in problems are in part the result of obvious differences in socioeconomic status. But a "problem" is the outcome of an act of definition on the part of an individual, and these judgments are culturally and ideologically conditioned. In recent years more attention has been given to the profound influence that people's beliefs, values and life styles have on their use of social services.[7] We shall pursue this in the next chapter; a few illustrations here will make the point.

In Walker's study of the clientele of the Roxbury Multi-Service Center and of the John F. Kennedy Center, he concluded that in addition to the observable differences in social and economic conditions faced by Charlestown's Irish-Americans and Roxbury's blacks, "the data reflected differences in perception of need between the two populations."[8]

If various groups define the same condition differently, then some will accept it and others will label it a problem with which they want help. Zola has suggested that even the symptoms of disease for which people seek medical help are defined by a person's culture, ethnic or reference group as relevant for action.[9]

[6] Lehmann, *op. cit.*, p. 96.

[7] See McKinlay's discussion of research on sociocultural factors, *op. cit.*, pp. 128–132.

[8] Walker, *op. cit.*, p. 92.

[9] See McKinlay's summary, *op. cit.*, p. 129.

The centers in the Bronx associated with Lincoln Hospital were ostensibly part of a community psychiatric service. However, Lehmann found that the percentage of psychiatric problems brought to the centers was not "impressive." He points out that people in that community seldom define their problems as psychiatric until they are severe and then they are referred to a physician or sometimes to the police.[10]

These culturally conditioned definitions are at the crux of much of the criticism which has been directed at social agencies. The critics insist that agencies and professionals lack an appreciation of the values and life style of lower class people. This division is reinforced by the fact that, in addition to social class differences, many consumers are black, Puerto Rican, Chicano or members of other minorities, while most professionals are white.

Agencies are condemned for trying to force people to abandon or change a viable, legitimate culture of their own. They are also damned for trying to get the client to "adjust to his situation," that is, for increasing the dependency of their clients and not helping them individually to change their circumstances or collectively to mobilize group pressure against bad housing, poor education, subsistence incomes, and inadequate health provisions.

The distaste for an "adjustment" approach to problems was linked to the emphasis that caseworkers and mental health personnel put on psychological factors. These practitioners were criticized on the grounds that they required their clients to be verbal and capable of self-examination, "middle class" qualities considered important in a therapeutic program based on the use of an interpersonal relationship. The question was asked whether the stress on psychological processes was as relevant in the ghettoes as efforts to modify environmental and economic pressures on their inhabitants.

There is evidence, most of it from the field of family service and the practice of social casework, that consumers and professionals indeed had disparate perceptions of what the former were bringing to the agencies. One study found that caseworkers and clients agreed on the principal problem in only 58 percent of the cases. Clients cited marital problems most often and economic and employment problems second; workers perceived personality problems of adults and marital problems most often, and economic and employment difficulties much less frequently than clients. "The client's tendency was often to locate the problem and the blame outside himself, while the worker tended to see the client himself as contributing significantly to his own problem . . ."[11]

There is a parallel to this difference in the way in which social agencies, which deal with many poor people, approach poverty as a problem. There are a number

[10] Lehmann, *op. cit.*, p. 95.

[11] Dorothy Fahs Beck, *Patterns in the Use of Family Agency Service*, New York: Family Service Association of America, 1962, p. 18.

of explanations for poverty. According to one view it stems from hostile social and economic conditions which crush the poor. Inadequate income, crumbling housing, and inferior slum schools grind people into a state of poverty and prevent their children from rising out of it. Another major explanation begins with the individual and the family and sees them not as people defeated by powerful external forces, but as victims of their own deficient mechanisms for coping with life and its opportunities.

Most social scientists explicitly and social welfare practitioners implicitly draw on these as well as other explanations of social problems. They believe that poverty is a thing of many causal strands that form a net in which the poor are caught and held fast. This assumption of multiple causes has been extended, in the realm of action, to mean that programs addressed to people in poverty must be prepared to deal with many factors and at the levels of individuals, families, and communities.

These dissimilar views about poverty furnish one example of the differing assumptions that are held by service consumers and providers. It is assumptions such as these, Briar and Miller point out, that bear on the dilemma of who is to determine the goals of service. An approach that is based on a "disease" model—a psychosocial "germ" theory—will call for professional expertise in setting goals and methods. A model that holds these problems to be stylistic and volitional, will give the consumer the responsibility and the right to decide.[12]

Most people do not grant an absolute right to either consumer or provider to establish the ends and the means of a helping process, but favor a collaboration. Assuming that cooperative exploration of possibilities has taken place, a strong case can be made at that point for accepting the client's decision concerning the form of help he is to receive. Handler and Hollingsworth argue in favor of this approach as a matter of legal entitlement when they recommend voluntary rather than compulsory use of social services by public welfare recipients.[13]

The matching of service to need *as defined by the professional worker* has now been challenged in several settings, as Rein points out.[14] The Gault decision of the Supreme Court removed professional judgment as the basis for determining the actions to be taken in cases of delinquency and called for a return to the basic legal process built on the adversary system. A study of workers in child welfare agencies showed that their recommendations concerning where a child should be placed were directly related to whether the worker was employed in

[12] Scott Briar and Henry Miller, *op. cit.*, p. 165.

[13] Joel F. Handler and Ellen Jane Hollingsworth, *The "Deserving Poor": A Study of Welfare Administration*, Institute for Research on Poverty Monograph Series, Chicago, Markham Publishing Company, 1971, p. 133.

[14] Martin Rein, *Social Policy*, New York, Random House, 1970. p. 130.

an agency that provided institutional care or one offering foster care, rather than on the client's need.

These questions are frequently complicated by raising psychological issues. It has been asked how can people, many of whom are confused and harassed at the time they seek help, know what they really want, much less what they need? Furthermore, their expressed request frequently masks deep-seated difficulties of which they may not even be aware.

This investigator rejects this approach to defining consumers problems. It may be true that the man who says he wants to find a job and the woman who wants a divorce have a number of difficulties which impinge on the problem being presented. It may also be true that the client, after contact with an agency, may broaden or redefine his problem. But, there are compelling reasons for accepting the client's "agenda," according to Reid, to avoid "fruitless and time-consuming efforts to engage semicaptive clients in helping relationships they have not asked for, do not want, and probably cannot use."[15]

Except for people who are clearly disoriented, we lack the diagnostic skills to determine, certainly on first contact, which statements represent "real" needs and which distort or conceal "the problem." From a pragmatic point of view, unless the social agency begins by confronting the problem as perceived by the consumer, the latter is likely to show his lack of confidence by voting with his feet and terminating the relationship.

In summary, a strong case can be made that in the giving and getting of social services, problems do indeed lie in the eye of the beholder. Whether the beholder is the consumer or the provider, his vision is affected by *cultural definitions* of what constitute problems which require help. Moreover, ideas about the causation of social and/or individual problems contribute to defining what should be done, that is, what the "need" is.

There is convincing evidence that the people who provide services and the consumers often see these things in very different ways. At the same time there is no single set of consumer perceptions of their problems and needs. We turn now to inquire into the variations among consumers.

---

[15] William J. Reid, "Target Problems, Time Limits, Task Structure," *Journal of Education for Social Work*, Vol. 8, No. 2, Spring 1972, p. 61.

3
Consumer Types

Differences in the ways that people perceive and act on their troubles are traceable, but only partly so, to the disparate conditions that they experience because of their race, age, sex or other sociodemographic characteristics. People who share these characteristics do not necessarily behave alike in their encounters with social agencies nor do they bring the same expectations. This recalls McKinlay's observation that although sociodemographic variables help to explain the behavior of some groups, they fail to account for differences among members of the same group.[1]

It is appropriate, therefore, to look at these behavioral differences among consumers of social services, and then to consider certain less tangible but significant variables—their values, beliefs, life-styles, and aspirations. The analysis of the data from the Roxbury center deals with two aspects of consumer behavior: the number of problems they presented to the RMSC staff and the frequency of their contacts with the agency.

A main assumption underlying the neighborhood centers was that people were burdened by many interlocking problems. There was evidence to support this. Cloward, Beck and others found that poor people did bring many problems to social agencies.[2] And the assumption was reinforced by action-research projects addressed to the "multiproblem family." This was defined as a family whose "disorganized social functioning" affected relationships within the family and neighborhood as well as the performance of tasks concerned with health, economic, and household practices designed to maintain the family as a unit.[3]

The corollary of the multiproblem concept was the assumption that effective programs must marshall an array of resources around the client. They were to be both comprehensive and coordinated. This stemmed from the widespread

---

[1] McKinlay, op. cit.

[2] Richard A. Cloward and Irwin Epstein, *Private Social Welfare's Disengagement from the Poor*, in Zald, op. cit., p. 625; Dorothy Fahs Beck, op. cit., p. 28. Beck reported that "lower class clients are somewhat more likely than upper class ones to have an overwhelmingly large number of problems." The report adds that people from the lowest social class had on the average four problems as perceived by their caseworkers and three according to the clients themselves.

[3] L.L. Geismar and Michael A. LaSorte, *Understanding the Multi-Problem Family: A Conceptual Analysis and Exploration in Early Identification*, New York: Association Press, 1964.

Table 5
Number of Clients' Problems Recorded at RMSC
In Percent

Number of Problems	Column A at Reception Desk (N = 3902)	Column B[a] at First Service (N = 2155)	Column C Final Count in Record (N = 2990)
1	77.7	52.7	28.8
2	16.1	28.7 ⎫	
3	4.7	12.6 ⎬	46.8
4+	1.5	5.9	23.7
	100.0	99.9	99.3

[a]The loss in numbers results from the lack of feedback from legal aid and to absence of recorded "second statements" for some additional clients.

criticism that social services are too narrowly defined, fragmented, and rigidly administered.

But how realistic was the initial assumption that people would present multiple problems? At the reception desk in Roxbury more than three-quarters of the people mentioned only one problem. At the other extreme, less than 2 percent spoke of four or more problems, as shown in Column A, Table 5.

At the point of entry the RMSC clients did not present multiple problems to the degree that had been expected. But that was the first presentation of their situation. Did this change in the course of their contacts with the Center and to what extent were additional problems articulated by clients or identified by the staff?

Two-thirds of the people for whom the information is available had *no increase* recorded in the number of their problems. Only one-fourth had one additional problem recorded after intake. In the end, as shown in Column C,

Table 6
Single and Multiple-Problem Clients by Race-Sex
In Percent
(N = 2717)

	Black Women	Black Men	White Women	White Men	Total
With single problems	40.5	51.4	30.8	42.9	43.0
With 2 or more problems	59.5	48.6	69.2	57.1	57.0

Table 7
Single and Multiple-Problem Clients by Age
In Percent
(N = 2908)

	Unknown	14–24	25–34	35–54	55–64	65+	Total
With single problems	48.0	53.1	40.2	35.8	48.4	38.8	43.9
With 2 or more problems	52.0	46.9	59.8	64.3	51.6	61.2	56.1

Table 5, approximately 30 percent of the clients still had only one problem noted in their record.

There are significant differences between this latter group and the multi-problem clients, both in their demographic characteristics and in the nature of their problems. Black men had single problems to a greater extent than the other race-sex groups and white women showed the highest percentage of multi-problem clients. Generally, the number of problems increased with age (see Tables 6 and 7).

The "problem profiles" of the two groups, presented in Table 8, show that employment-related difficulties account for almost half the single problems but only one-fifth of the difficulties of the multiproblem clients. Family, financial, and health problems are more prominent among those people who had a number of difficulties.

Table 8
Distribution of Problems Among
Single- and Multiproblem Clients
In Percent

Nature of Problem	Single-Problem[1] Clients	Multiproblem[2] Clients
Employment	46.9	20.3
Family	14.6	24.0
Housing	13.1	15.8
Welfare and financial	10.7	19.6
Training and education	10.1	9.3
Health	4.5	11.0
	99.9	100.0

[1]$N = 1805$. 74 information requests and 47 legal problems have been omitted.

[2]$N = 4796$. 100 information requests and 232 legal problems have been omitted.

It is possible that people mentioned more problems than were recorded. It would be understandable to record the problems on which action was taken or contemplated and not to record those that the worker did not intend to deal with immediately or at all. But it is not likely that more complete recording would alter our finding. We would still be challenged to explain the variability among clients and, in particular, to understand why a considerable proportion of people apparently sought help with only one problem.

Considering the nature of ghetto life, it is probable that many of the people who appear in the records as "single-problem clients" were in fact experiencing difficulties in several areas of living. Why then did so many of them decide to focus their problem presentation on a single need? What these people did, of course, runs counter to the tendency of many professionals to think and act in terms of "the whole person and the whole family" or "the total situation."

It is possible that the group about whom we are speculating is more realistic and practical, and that they limited their request to what they thought was achievable. They may have eschewed those complex problems about which they sensed not much could be done. This is in accord with what Briar found in his study of AFDC applicants who went to the welfare agency for financial aid and nothing else.[4] They found the caseworkers' inquiries about other matters to be irrelevant and irritating.

Some of the people at the RMSC may have narrowed their problem presentation because of the urgency of their need. This was undoubtedly the case with many of those who had job-related problems and who turned out to be "single-problem" clients. It is understandable that they would not be eager to explore other, perhaps less pressing problems simultaneously. But this assumption is not completely warranted because even more people with employment difficulties appear in the records as multiproblem clients.

The way people presented themselves in terms of the number of problems they articulated is closely associated with another aspect of their behavior—the frequency of their contacts with the agency.[5]

The number of contacts at the RMSC varied from a substantial group with a single contact to a few who had 100, 150 and, in one instance, 179 contacts during the 27 months under review.

As Table 9 indicates, black men had fewer contacts than the other race-sex groups; women had more contacts. Younger people—especially those with employment needs—came less often (See Table 10). The people who came most

---

[4] Briar and Miller, op. cit., p. 95.

[5] There was a requirement at the Roxbury Center that workers fill out a "contact form" after every event with or on behalf of a client. Of the 13,259 client contacts recorded involving 2861 clients, 41.6 percent were interviews at the Center and 20.0 percent were home visits. In addition, 31.3 percent were telephone calls. The remainder of 7.1 percent were letters and escort services.

Table 9
Characteristics of Clients by Number of Contacts with RMSC
In Percent

	Number of Contacts		
	1–2	3–5	6+
Race-sex (N = 2866)			
Black Women	57.9	60.8	71.2
Black Men	32.7	31.4	17.8
White Women	6.8	4.8	9.1
White Men	2.6	3.0	2.0
Age (N = 2811)			
14–24	41.0	35.3	26.6
25–34	27.7	28.8	34.3
35–54	25.9	30.2	34.4
55–64	3.4	3.9	2.9
65+	1.9	1.9	1.9
Marital status (N = 2179)			
Married	32.0	38.2	38.7
[a]Separated	29.3	30.4	39.6
Never Married	38.7	31.4	21.7
No. of children (N = 2310)			
None	32.6	30.9	16.7
1	18.0	17.0	14.6
2	16.5	16.1	16.9
3–4	20.1	20.1	26.8
5+	12.9	15.9	25.0
Years of education (N = 2327)			
0–8	30.4	39.5	50.5
9+	69.6	60.5	49.5

[a]Includes widowed and divorced.

frequently had more problems concerning their families, their health, and their finances.

One might have anticipated that problems of family functioning and personal adjustment would entail fairly frequent contact with the Center. By the same token one could expect, given the extent of unemployment among black men and the difficulty of finding jobs for them, that they would not return over and over to a place where most of them could not find work. This would help to explain why, in general, black men had fewer contacts than black women or whites.

Frequency of problems and frequency of contacts with the agency are closely related, as Figure 1 makes evident.

Table 10
Clients' Problems and Frequency of Contact with RMSC
In Percent

| | Number of Contacts | | |
Nature of Problem	1−2	3−5	6+
Employment	38.0	31.7	12.9
Family	15.4	16.4	28.5
Housing	13.6	13.1	13.7
Financial	12.4	14.0	18.5
Education	7.5	11.4	8.1
Health	7.3	9.5	13.8
Legal	5.7	4.0	4.5
	99.9	100.1	100.0

The high correlation between number of contacts and number of problems is reinforced by the data in Table 11.

A picture of differential use of services is emerging from this analysis. The factors that are coalescing include the demographic characteristics of the

Figure 1. Distribution of RMSC clients by number of contacts and number of problems.

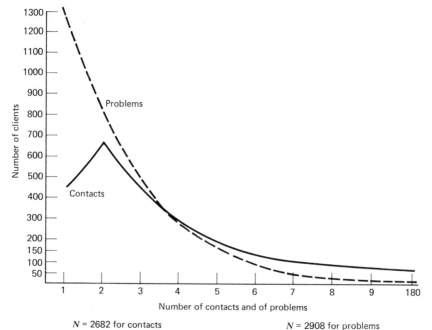

N = 2682 for contacts N = 2908 for problems

Table 11
Distribution of RMSC Clients by
Number of Contacts and Problems

Number of Problems in Client's Record	Number of Contacts			Total (Percent)
	1-2	3-5	6+	
1	A 55.9	24.2	9.0	28.8
	55.9	34.7	9.4	861
2-3	37.0	B 59.0	39.5	46.8
	22.8	51.9	25.3	1400
4+	4.9	16.7	C 51.3	23.7
	5.9	29.1	65.0	708
Total	28.8	41.2	30.0	
	842	1232	895	2969[a]

Upper cell entries are percent of column totals.

Lower entries are percent of row totals.

[a]Twenty-one cases coded as having "no problem" have been omitted from the table.

individual, the nature and number of problems he presents, and the frequency of his contacts. There is a group of consumers (in Cell A) who presented one problem and had limited contact with the RMSC. A sizable percentage of black men, with their focus on employment needs, falls into this category.

There is a second group of people with very frequent contact and multiple problems, among whom we should expect to find black women in considerable numbers, with their interrelated concerns about family, finances, housing, and employment. They appear in Cell C.

The interweaving of ethnic factors, the nature of the person's problem, and the frequency of his contact with an agency is well illustrated by this observation from the centers in the Bronx.

> The centers, on the other hand, are better able to cope with Puerto Rican problems of family and finances (financial problems frequently concern legitimate claims to welfare benefits) than with the black's need for employment and better housing. Possibly as a result, blacks are more likely to make a single visit, while Puerto Ricans return for multiple visits.[6]

But it would be a mistake to place too much emphasis on race-sex as determining factors. Black men and black women, as well as whites, appear in Cells A and C, as well as in Cell B that represents those with a few problems who "invested" more than one or two contacts with the RMSC but not nearly as many as the second group.

[6] Lehmann, op. cit., p. 96.

It is our speculation that these variations are also linked to the less tangible factors of belief, value, and life style and that these play an important part in the expectations and behavior of social service consumers. Increasingly students of "psychological economics" are turning to these factors. Strumpel writes, for example:

> People's productive behavior and their satisfactions are assumed to be shaped by goals or values (what do people want?), reality perceptions and expectations (how do they evaluate their situation in relation to their goals?), and self-efficacy/fate-control (to what extent are they confident of their ability to move closer to their goals?).[7]

This is not to deny the place of psychological and emotional factors in the behavior of social service consumers, nor the fact that these cut across many of the variables discussed in this study. Personality differences and psychological elements interact with values and attitudes in shaping the behavior of individuals. These have been studied in the social services to a greater extent than the variables with which this study is primarily concerned.

Take, for example, the optimism or pessimism with which people approach a troublesome circumstance in their lives, or the extent to which they want to preserve their autonomy or are willing to be dependent on others in dealing with a problem. These factors will have much weight in determining whether people seek out social services as a source of assistance, what their expectations will be, and how much of an investment of their time, energy, and other resources they are willing to make.[8]

A number of factors such as optimism-pessimism and autonomy-dependency can be significant in consumer-provider interactions and can differentiate among consumers. Since many consumers are poor people, it is useful to look for these factors in the studies that have been done on poverty, beginning with the controversial idea of a "culture of poverty." Oscar Lewis, the chief proponent of the concept, conceived of the culture of poverty as a design for living that serves as an adaptive function for *some* of the poor in capitalist, cash-based economies, regardless of their racial or ethnic background.[9]

Lewis describes the people who share this culture as disengaged from the major institutions of society which they view with fear, suspicion, and apathy. In terms of community there is much gregariousness but a minimum of

[7] Burkhard Strumpel, "Economic Life-Styles, Values, and Subjective Welfare-An Empirical Approach," in Eleanor Bernert Sheldon, ed. *Family Economic Behavior: Problems and Prospects,* New York: J.B. Lippincott, 1973, p. 71.

[8] See Gerald Gurin and Patricia Gurin, "Expectance Theory in the Study of Poverty," *Journal of Social Issues,* 26, No. 2, 1970.

[9] Oscar Lewis, "The Culture of Poverty," *Scientific American,* October 1966.

organization. The family tends to be mother-centered and individuals grow up with strong feelings of fatalism, helplessness, dependence, and inferiority.

If this description were applicable to the people who used the center in Roxbury, one could predict that their behavior as social service consumers would be generally similar, and that their attitudes would probably be characterized by distrust and hopelessness toward the RMSC as a source of help. A reading of the RMSC case records does not support those predictions. On the contrary, it challenges the notion of a homogeneous culture among the residents of a community such as Roxbury.

The experience in Roxbury and elsewhere leads rather toward a recognition of heterogeneity among poor people. While some of the RMSC users fit Oscar Lewis' description, many others do not. Their picture of themselves and their attitudes and behavior toward the RMSC can best be described by the writings of Hylan Lewis, S. M. Miller, Herbert Gans, Lee Rainwater, Walter Miller and others who stress differences among the poor and within the lower class.

This literature is suggestive of the factors that bear on people's behavior as consumers of social services. Three such "focal concerns" are cited here from the work of Walter Miller.[10] One theme concerns *fate* and the conviction that a person's life is subject to forces beyond his control, thus making it futile to take the initiative or to "plan" to improve his situation. Closely related is the issue of *autonomy* and the desire, often ambivalent, to be free of external constraints, but at the same time wanting to be cared for by a strong authority. Third is what Miller calls "*smartness*," the capacity to outwit others in order to obtain a desired end.

But these elements are by no means limited to the poor; they can be elaborated to describe a broad range of social service consumers, regardless of social class. Thus, one might add to Miller's list.

1. The dimension, noted earlier, of *optimism-pessimism.*

2. The degree of *passivity* or *assertiveness* with which a person interacts with others.

3. The extent of *conceptualization and verbalization* as against an orientation to *nonverbal communication* and *physical action.*

These and other characteristics and values surface in the encounters between consumers and providers of social services. This perspective was sensitively applied by Mayer and Timms in their research on the reactions of working class clients to case-work treatment in an English agency.[11] Their chief interest was in client satisfaction and dissatisfaction.

---

[10] Walter B. Miller, "Lower Class Culture as a Generating Milieu of Gang Delinquency," *Journal of Social Issues*, March 1958.

[11] John E. Mayer and Noel Timms, *The Client Speaks: Working Class Impressions of Casework*, New York, Atherton Press, 1970.

One group of clients, those seeking help with interpersonal problems, were dissatisfied when treated by workers who were "insight-oriented" and who did not meet the clients' expectation that the worker would fix the "blame" on someone, or would give them straightforward advice.

Other clients, also seeking help with interpersonal problems, were satisfied by workers who were "supportive-directive" and who conveyed more warmth and offered guidance. Mayer and Timms speculate that some of the satisfied clients may also have defined problems and problem-solving more nearly like the workers, that is in middle class terms.

The other group of clients Mayer and Timms studied came for assistance with material problems. Those who were satisfied felt so, for the most part, because they received what they wanted, plus nonmaterial benefits such as emotional support or relief through unburdening themselves. Other clients in this group were dissatisfied, primarily because they did not receive the material assistance they came for.

The expectations of the people in Mayer and Timms' study reflect variations in style, belief, and values that differentiate users of social services. There are grounds for relating these differences to the patterns of consumer behavior discussed in this chapter—the people who brought many problems and had frequent and extended contact with the Roxbury center; those who presented one or two sharply-focused problems and came only once or twice; a third group of people who fall in between the other two in terms of the problems they presented and the frequency of their contacts with the agency.

The nature of the requests made of the RMSC by these three groupings differed and it seems reasonable to suppose that their expectations differed as did their outlooks on the world and on themselves. We find patterns here that can be explained by conceiving of the three types of consumers described in the next chapter.

4

Mrs. Burgess, Mrs. Perkins, and Mrs. Rogers

People come to social agencies with differing problems and expectations and they vary in the intensity of their use of the agencies. In the previous chapter we speculated that these variations are related to values, beliefs, aspirations, and life-styles. Based on these speculations, we present here a typology of social service consumers, illustrated through cases drawn from the Roxbury Multi-Service Center.

The scheme consists of three main types.

1. The "buffeted" people who brought multiple problems to the RMSC and came over and over again in search of help are represented by Mrs. Burgess in the descriptions that follow.

2. The "problem-solvers" who presented a few difficulties with which they wanted assistance and for which they were willing to contact the RMSC more than once or twice but not nearly as often as the first group. Mrs. Perkins illustrates this type.

3. The "resource-seekers" who focused on one or two problems and "invested" only a few contacts with the Center. Mrs. Rogers exemplifies these people.

This three-part typology builds on the work of John Douds and Phyllis Silverman, who each suggested three models of lower class, black consumers of social services.[1] There is a close similarity between two of the types they

[1] John J. Douds, "Client Types and Differential Use of a Multi-Service System: The Coper, The Striver, The Hard Core," unpublished paper, 1967, The Florence Heller Graduate School for Advanced Studies in Social Welfare, Brandeis University, Waltham, Mass.

Phyllis Rolfe Silverman, *The Client Who Drops Out: A Study of Spoiled Helping Relationships*, unpublished doctoral dissertation, 1968, The Florence Heller Graduate School for Advanced Studies in Social Welfare, Brandeis University, Waltham, Mass.

proposed and this thinking has been incorporated in what we call "the buffeted" and the "problem-solvers." Our third type departs from Silverman's typology and to some extent from Douds'.

It must be borne in mind that these are "ideal types," that is, they are abstractions not found in "pure" form in flesh and blood. The types represent tendencies in thinking and behavior rather than literally and utterly different groups of people.[2] Moreover, the tendency of a particular individual should not be considered fixed. Over time his orientation may shift from one type to another. The fact that no person corresponds in every respect to the ideal type is apparent in the descriptions of three RMSC clients that are presented here.

Our objective in setting forth this typology is to focus attention on the consumer and, in particular, on the expectations and wishes concerning the service that he brings to a social agency. Whether expectations are fulfilled or thwarted is a crucial question for all consumers. That we may be dealing with quite disparate expectations among consumers is a matter that requires further study. We begin with Mrs. Burgess.[3]

THE "BUFFETED"

Mrs. Burgess came to the Center at the suggestion of a worker in the welfare department because she wanted to obtain a legal separation. The Burgesses, both 39 years old, have been married 21 years and have eight children, the oldest at home being 18.

For the past six years there has been a history of marital conflict, sporadic dependence on welfare, Mr. Burgess' heavy drinking, and physical violence on his part. He works, but rarely, as an odd-jobs man in construction but has no sought-after skills. The family has moved frequently and has often been in arrears in rent. Charges against the 14-year-old girl for shoplifting are pending in Juvenile Court.

Two years ago Mrs. Burgess filed a non-support complaint against her husband. He was referred at the time for psychiatric treatment but did not follow up on it. After seeing the lawyer at the RMSC, Mrs. Burgess and then Mr. Burgess acquiesced in the recommendation that they try marital counseling. One caseworker held weekly sessions with Mrs. Burgess designed to help her clarify and understand her own emotions and behavior and her ambivalence about her husband, reflected in the fact that repeatedly she calls the police to have him removed from the home but later accepts him back.

[2] See Jerome Cohen's cautions on this point in Reissman et al., *Mental Health of the Poor*, op. cit., p. 130.

[3] This account is excerpted from the records and from interviews Phyllis Silverman conducted with the RMSC client and a worker. Names and other means of identifying the persons have been disguised (see Silverman, op. cit.).

Another caseworker met a few times with Mr. Burgess but the latter soon withdrew from this. An Employment Counselor in the Center discussed training with him and referred him to several jobs but as a result of absenteeism and drinking, these jobs never lasted more than a few days.

Mrs. Burgess continued to find life unbearable and on many occasions kept asking for a separation. She told her caseworker that she was not finding the counseling useful. Though Mrs. Burgess said it was comforting to talk with the caseworker, there was no chance for success since Mr. Burgess was not cooperating. Mrs. Burgess also began drinking heavily, especially after an episode between her husband and another woman in the Burgess' home. The oldest boy defended his mother against his father on many occasions.

At the end of a one-month stay in jail, the RMSC staff intervened on Mr. Burgess' behalf, urged that he be placed on probation and promised every cooperation in a treatment plan. The court psychiatrist also approved probation and urged Mr. Burgess to return to the church and to get help from AA. But the situation continued to deteriorate. Mrs. Burgess terminated her contacts with her RMSC caseworker, but turned up frequently at the welfare office with requests for money and other kinds of concrete help. The welfare worker had originally referred Mrs. Burgess to the RMSC because she had felt helpless and unable to be of assistance to the family.

A second review conference was held,[4] this time involving the RMSC consulting psychiatrist, the Probation Officer, the Employment Counselor, and supervisory personnel from the Center. Although he was unable to attend, the court psychiatrist recommended that Mr. Burgess be incarcerated, preferably at a state prison where he might be able to receive psychiatric treatment, since the controls possible under probation were not sufficient. The RMSC psychiatrist concurred.

The Probation Officer stated that if Mr. Burgess were physically able to work but was unable to hold a job because of his drinking, then the Court would incarcerate him at Deer Island. There he would receive no psychiatric treatment or vocational training. He went on to say that there is no prison that has a treatment program for alcoholics. He said he would give Mr. Burgess four weeks to find and hold a job.

The three oldest children went to the welfare worker to say that the home situation was impossible with both parents constantly drunk and fighting and that they were fearful about the health and welfare of the younger children.

The last entry in the record, except for some references to unsuccessful attempts to contact the family, reports that Mrs. Burgess told the welfare worker her husband was not contributing to the support of the family, was

---

[4] "Review Conference" was the term used for an interagency case conference. In addition to dealing with a specific case, the RMSC staff used these occasions to educate and to press other agencies into new practices and methods.

breaking in at night, staying over, and leaving in the morning. It was left that
Mrs. Burgess would write a letter to that effect to the Probation Officer.

The Burgess family shares a way of life and an outlook with other people who came again and again and again to the Roxbury Center, a way of life that consists essentially of a harsh struggle for survival against a fate that seems inexorable. Of the three types, they are the most hard-pressed, the most crisis-ridden, and the most devoid of hope. They come the closest to Lewis' description of the "culture of poverty."

S.M. Miller refers to them as "the unstable," living in chronic dependency, the victims of poor physical health, mental, familial, and personal instability; prolonged unemployment; and low income.[5] Silverman calls them "the defeated" and found them to be mostly in female-headed households, where parents and children left school at an early age, where unions are temporary, pregnancies frequently occur out of wedlock, and where households are disorganized and dirty and the days appear to lack a plan.[6]

This group consists essentially of the multiproblem families first identified in 1952 by Buell and his associates in the St. Paul project.[7] They were found to comprise only six percent of the families in the community but more than half of the community's health and welfare services were devoted to their care. Lagey and Ayres describe these families as seriously disorganized, and accounting for a disproportionate share of deviant behavior, such as abuse and neglect of children, juvenile delinquency, adult crime, and adult alcoholism.[8] Oscar Lewis comments, however, that social scientists writing about multiproblem families stress their disorganization while he has found their behavior "clearly patterned and reasonably predictable."[9]

These are the people who seem to be caught in a windstorm in which everything is loose, flying about, an imminent threat to life itself. They are

[5] S.M. Miller, "The American Lower Classes: A Typological Approach," reprinted from *Social Research*, 1964, in Frank Reissman, *Mental Health of the Poor*, p. 146—147.

[6] Silverman, op. cit.

[7] Bradley Buell and Associates, *Community Planning for Human Services* (New York: Columbia University Press, 1952); Benjamin Schlesinger, *The Multi-Problem Family: A Review and Annotated Bibliography* (Toronto: University of Toronto Press, 1963); Joseph C. Lagey and Beverly Ayres, *Community Treatment Programs for Multi-Problem Families* (Vancouver, B.C.: Community Chest and Councils of the Greater Vancouver Area, 1962); and Scott Briar, "Family Services," op. cit., for a review and critique of research in this field.

[8] Lagey and Ayres, op. cit., p. 16.

[9] Lewis, op. cit.

indeed "the buffeted" of our society, seeking protection but fearful and suspicious. When troubles strike, they have little leverage but to react by using their "smartness," to try to manipulate the social institutions that seem to be manipulating them.

Silverman found in her interviews that direct confrontation of a problem through talk makes them feel sick and more helpless. Talking is to unburden oneself, not a means to get at the nature of one's problem. A person will resort to force to deal with some problems, for example, in the management of their children. This is done not out of hateful impulses, but out of helplessness in not knowing how to discipline or restrain them. They depend heavily on relatives, friends, and agencies for advice, even for decisions.

We encountered the buffeted people in the RMSC data as the clients with the most problems and the most contacts with the Center. In comparison with the two other groups, they had the highest percentage of women and people in the 25–54 age group. They had more children and were more likely to be widowed, separated or divorced and to have had less education. Relative to the other groups they had more difficulties in the areas of welfare, finances, family, health, and problems with the schools.

THE PROBLEM-SOLVER*

I had no money and I had to quit my job because I had to stay home and take care of the children. After the baby was born my husband started acting real crazy. He was drinking and carrying on. I had an elderly woman caring for the children and I could not have her any more. My salary was not enough. When I went to the Center they assigned me to a Social Worker and she got in touch with Welfare. They gave me a slip and I bought food and paid the rent.

Then I took the M.D.T.A. course and got money from that. I was taking a clerk-typist course and was in school from 3 in the afternoon to 9:30. I never did work in that kind of job. I started to work in a pre-school program as a Neighborhood Aide. The Multi-Service Center arranged for that.

The Social Worker talks to me like I'm a human being. She sent two of my children to a camp in Maine for the summer. And then they started to work with the twelve-year old who was emotionally disturbed. They sent him to a

*Mrs. Perkins looks younger than her 41 years. She has six children ranging in age from 17 years to 16 months. This is her second marriage. She has had three years of college and a nursery training course and is now waiting for a course in Early Childhood Development. She lives in a wooden three-decker, which is in disrepair. Her living room has old but substantial furniture covered in plastic slipcovers and one easy chair of modern design.

This account is exerpted from interviews Phyllis Silverman conducted with the client and the RMSC worker. See Silverman, *op. cit.*

psychiatrist and they've just got him into a special school. He's an extremely nervous boy. He can't learn. He's three grades behind. He's had a block. He's immature. I've been aware of this but I didn't know what to do about it. I had him on the waiting list at Mass. General but their list is years long. But through the Multi-Service Center we were able to push things right along.

The school he's going to is a small school where they give you a lot of individual attention. In public school he was in a special class for three years where they never did anything. They painted and they were always having some shop work to do but that's all. He knew nothing about history or geography or reading. I don't care how slow a child may be, but I think he should know something about these things. In fact he happens to be a very smart boy. These children have to be taught in a certain way and that cannot be done if there are too many children in the class. And then the teachers are not equipped to train these children. I knew he was overly protected. I always had elderly people caring for him and there was one woman who didn't let anyone even breathe on him.

Now the Multi-Service Center is helping me with my fourteen-year old boy. He's had problems but he had a bad fall when he was a little child. He stayed in the hospital for four months after that and the doctor told me that a change would take place when he started school. He had awful headaches and sometimes it would be so bad that he would bang his head and sometimes he would have nosebleeds all night. He's five foot ten and he thinks that no one should hit him but me. He minds me but at school he won't mind anybody else. He gets in with the other boys who are pretty rough kids. The Center promised to get him a job and they will send him to camp this summer.

We first took him to Mass. General when he was seven and when he started to have trouble in school. The school sent him to the language clinic; they thought he needed remedial reading and work that he could get there, but they also thought that he needed the treatment as well. So they sent him to Family Service. They worked with him three times a week. He was withdrawn and he didn't like to play rough games. They meant to bring him out, so that he would participate more in things. They wanted to find out what was bothering him—I think through play.

As for getting help from the Social Worker at the Center, well, you can talk to someone you don't know; they are more objective. A friend is more prejudiced. She's going to say you're right even if you're wrong because she knows you.

I think a person has all the control that he might want over his own life. I had always hoped that I would have lots of children. I was the only child, and sure enough, I did. Yes, I think planning does some good. You mean for children? Oh yes, because I want the best for my children, that's what I'm trying to do.

By comparison with the "buffeted people," Mrs. Perkins and the other "problem-solvers" have (or like to believe they have) greater economic security and brighter prospects. Equipped with more education and better job skills, responsible for fewer children, and with a longer history of being urbanized, they strive to be "respectable" and middle class, even though they may be on welfare and, in reality, facing the same pervasive problems of the ghetto that others do.

Their homes are tidy, if threadbare. But housekeeping is far less important than the social and economic advancement of their families. They are deeply agitated over the dangers and temptations of the life around them in which they feel trapped, but they do not believe that these conditions are the result of immovable forces. They hope and plan to escape the ghetto (or at least its impact on their lives) through their own efforts by way of education, skilled jobs, and if possible by moving to "better neighborhoods." While they remain in the ghetto they are willing to act in concert with others to improve conditions. They hope to accomplish this by upgrading the institutions that bear on their lives.

They approach their personal problems and the problems of the community as matters of rational planning leading to action. In these efforts, the experts and professionals, far from being feared, are to be enlisted as allies. They have a strong sense of autonomy. And while they want to cooperate with professionals, they also want respect from them. They can be critical of professionals when they do not measure up.

The problem-solvers believe that life's pleasures should be taken within the framework of middle class morality and the law, though this is not always possible. Since they live above the elemental level of the survival struggle that typifies the "buffeted," they can afford to be concerned with psychological security and well-being. They often blame themselves and feel guilty about their children. They are given to more introspection and to the cultivation of their own capacities for functioning more rationally and effectively.

The problem-solvers correspond to RMSC clients with a moderate number of problems and contacts. Compared with the "buffeted" clients, they had twice as many men among them, were younger by a few years, and included families with fewer children, more husbands in the family, and more education. Their "problem profiles" resembled that of the "buffeted" people except that they came much more often to seek jobs and training.

THE RESOURCE-SEEKERS*

When I went to the Multi-Service Center I was living at Number 38 Ames. The housing was very bad. I had heard no complaint from the landlord but

*This account is a condensation of a record at the RMSC. Mrs. Rogers is 31. Her four children live with her. They have been on AFDC for four years. She is a quiet, soft-spoken woman with a heavy Southern accent who seems articulate in her own slow, decisive way.

the neighbors said he was evicting people. And although I didn't hear that I was being evicted I got worried. So I first went to the Multi-Service Center to see if I was going to be evicted. I heard that if you went to the Multi-Service Center they would take care of these problems, so I went down.

They came out to see the house. They wanted to know how much rent I was paying. I was paying $80 a month there. They sent me to the housing downtown to apply for the project. They sent a letter and I did get into the Columbia Point project and I said I didn't want to go out there. I have a sick child and I would have no way of getting transportation if she needed to go to the hospital and I have heard not good things about that place. And they said they would keep my name on file and I haven't heard anything. I found this place through my sister-in-law who lives next door.

I heard about the Multi-Service Center from a friend who was one of the first clients there when they first opened. She said to go down there and they would tell me what to do. I was so upset. I do have four kids and the landlord could just come and tell me to get out. My friend said that they do good, that they liked to help you and that they're good. She goes there now when she has a problem. I found them good too.

They helped me from worrying. They talked to the landlord and he didn't say anything about my being evicted. They told me where to go to find out about the projects because I didn't know where to go. When you went to Welfare I had to tell my life's story. But up at Multi-Service Center they just did not ask a whole lot of questions about my personal business. Yes, I say in order for someone to help you they ought to know about you. They want to know if you're paying the rent and I told them that I held back the rent because the landlord hadn't fixed the apartment, that I had the money and I would give it to him as soon as it was 'fixed'.

I noticed that there was Legal Aid in there and I went in to talk to them about a divorce. He told me that I needed $35 to start anything. I could pay $35 now and $30 later. But I didn't have the money at that time. Sometimes I have $15 saved up and I say I'm going to put it away for that, and then some bill comes along and I pay it and I don't have the money.

My marriage didn't work out because my husband didn't provide. The last fight we had we wound up in court and that's when the judge told us we'd be better off if we separated. . . . I think every kid wants and should have a father. My son is a big boy; when he was small I could sit and talk to him but now he's big and he can't ask me things. He can ask my boy-friend and he'll listen to him and even though he knows he is not his father, he gets along with him.

You know I want to get married again but in a way I'm scared. I don't know if marrying him I'll get along. I'm afraid if I get the divorce I'll get pushed into getting married. We've been going together for four years. I talked about this with the social worker at Welfare but I never thought about getting help with this at the Multi-Service.

They asked me to come back to the Multi-Service if I ever have problems. But I didn't. I didn't even change my address there which I will if I have to go for another problem or to the lawyer. I was going to see about getting the children into camp but then I don't think they wanted to go, so I passed that by.

A lady from the Multi-Service, not the one I saw there, came to my house once and asked about my kids and do I have trouble with my teen-age boy running the street. I don't have that kind of problem. Bills are a problem that I have. I'm always short of money.

I might talk to my sister-in-law if I had a problem but generally I don't talk to anyone. I don't think talking does any good . . . I guess I just bear with my problems. Sometimes they pass over. I sometimes speak to the guy I'm engaged to. If I have financial problems I mention it to him and he gives me money. I find myself getting along all right.

One does not find the resource-seeker described in the literature on social class, culture, and stratification. However, the data from Roxbury point strongly toward this type of consumer. About 30 percent of the RMSC users narrowly limited their problem presentation at the Center and invested only one or two contacts to see whether they could get what they wanted.

By comparison with the problem-solvers and the buffeted clients, they were younger, more of them unmarried, and markedly better educated. Men comprised one-third of this grouping. Employment was the outstanding need, accounting for almost half the problems they brought. They came least often in connection with their health.

This grouping contains, to a greater extent than the others, young married couples who face the economic pressures that accompany family formation—the acquisition of housing, the purchase of furniture, the medical and other expenses that come with the first child. In terms of the family life cycle, they are struggling to cope with the "resource gap" that many low income families face at this stage.

The distinctive ideas and behavior of the resource-seekers are related to what Walter Miller called "smartness," the ability to maneuver around obstacles, take the initiative, and succeed in getting what one is after. This may also be related to the tough, action-oriented style that is found in descriptions of working class culture.

This assertiveness contrasts with the greater passivity of the buffeted people. The resource-seeker is more aggressive in his bargaining and in his demands. Rainwater describes such a woman in the Pruitt-Igoe housing project in St. Louis. She managed "to make the bureaucracies produce the basic resources she needed for herself and her family and to ward off their incursions on her family's autonomy."[10] Unlike the problem-solvers, this type of person does not engage in efforts at self-examination and improvement of problem-solving skills. Their stance is essentially pragmatic, antiintellectual and antiprofessional.

[10] Rainwater, op. cit., p. 211.

Another typology, drawn from a study of mothers of retarded children and their encounters with the medical care system, delineates patterns that converge and overlap with the types suggested here.[11] Schwartz projects three consumer strategies: passive acceptance, active questing, and withdrawal from medical care.

The basic stance of the first of these ideal types is an acceptance of professionals' authority and their definition of the situation. The mother seeks to accommodate to the helper's judgment of what is best for the retarded child and for the family, and to the professional's way of structuring the helping relationship. The parent assumes a relationship of unequal knowledge and power. While the total life situation of the buffeted consumers in this book may differ from the parents in the Schwartz study, the expectations and behavior of the passive-acceptance type and of the buffeted have much in common.

The active-questing mothers want their relationships with professionals "to involve a mutual accommodating of perspectives with joint decision-making in the areas in which the parent feels qualified." The parents' rationale is that the decisions to be made are not necessarily technical or medical, but often rest on preferences, values, and life-styles. Since the mother knows her family better than the professional and has more to gain or lose, she sees the provider as recommending diagnoses and treatment plans, but open to exploration of their consequences and of alternatives. The overlap with the problem-solvers is apparent.

Schwartz' third type withdraws from contact with medical care providers instead of accepting the professional's direction. These parents are unwilling to negotiate a more satisfactory treatment plan. It is not known to what extent these mothers were ready or able—in the manner of the resource-seekers—to look elsewhere for help.

It is also interesting to note some parallels in a study of paraprofessional workers conducted by Kramer at the Roxbury Multi-Service Center.[12] Using Merton's concepts of "locals" and "cosmopolitans," Kramer describes a group he calls "the homeowners." Well rooted in thier neighborhood, they are interested mostly in achieving some immediate benefit for clients rather than in long-range planning, institutional change or social movements.

The "hometowners" views the agency as a means of "assistance for his fellow neighbors, who are currently not being serviced properly by the bureaucratic institutions." He is likely to be older, married, less schooled, less aspiring and less militant than the other types. The characteristics Kramer attributes to the

[11] Charlotte Green Schwartz, "Strategies and Tactics of Mothers of Mentally Retarded Children for Dealing with the Medical Care System," in Norman R. Bernstein, M.D., ed., *Diminished People—the Problems and Care of the Mentally Retarded,* Little, Brown & Co., 1970.

"hometowner" come very close to describing the "resource-seeker" in the typology presented above.

Kramer's second type, "the striver," is middle-class oriented. Compared to the "hometowner" he has more education, is occupationally more ambitious, and identifies with the professional workers in the agency. He is active in community-wide and city-wide organizations. If the "hometowner" is parochial, the "striver" is "ecumenical" and cosmopolitan. The resemblance to Mrs. Perkins and the "problem-solvers" is apparent. The third type in Kramer's scheme, the militant, social-action oriented "activist," has no explicit parallel among the RMSC consumers.

Each of the types of consumers described in this chapter has a distinct set of expectations and a particular way of seeking and using the assistance of social agencies. Their expectations of social agencies are shown in Table 12. The intensity of each expectation or need, in comparison with other expectations held by the same person, is indicated by the number of check marks.

Table 12
Consumer Expectations of Agency Service

	The Buffeted	Resource- Seekers	Problem- Solvers
Information, linkage		XXX	X
Direct, material assistance	XXX	XXX	X
Emotional support	XX		X
Advice	XX		XXX
Self-understanding			XXX
Advocacy	XXX	X	X

The extent to which the expectations of people like Mrs. Burgess, Mrs. Rogers and Mrs. Perkins were fulfilled in their encounters with the Roxbury Center is the subject of Chapter 5.

5

Expectations – Fulfilled and Frustrated

By no means do all people who approach social agencies find the assistance they seek. Some are helped; some are not; some are lost and forgotten in a bewildering maze of social welfare organizations. To raise these questions about the outcome and effectiveness of agency activities is to step into murky water. The definition and measurement of improvements or "successes" have long been matters of uncertainty and debate. The criteria for successful outcomes are difficult to come by, mostly because the specific objectives of service are seldom delineated clearly at the outset.

The planners of the Roxbury Multi-Service Center tried to avoid this impasse by asking the staff to record at the close of the first contact with each client "what changes will be sought?" This information was not recorded consistently enough to use the answers in assessing results. Instead, assessors, independent of the RMSC and working under the supervision of a social scientist and a social worker, made judgments based on their reading of the records. These outcome assessments applied to the client's condition as a whole and not to specific problems.[1] However, in addition, a separate determination was made of *each problem* to see whether it had been handled within the RMSC, by referral to another agency, or by no action being taken.

Slightly better than one-third of the clients had positive outcomes—9 percent had "important" results and 28 percent had "some" results. These men and

[1] The assessors had six choices.

1. No action was attempted by the RMSC service responsible.
2. The client stopped coming; no results achieved.
3. The worker stopped service or termination was jointly agreed, with no results achieved.
4. Some results were achieved.
5. Significant or important results were achieved.
6. Referred but no information on follow-up.

Outcomes were assessed for 3025 clients. The 1036 missing observations consisted almost entirely of persons referred to Legal Service whose files were not part of the central record system.

Table 13

Outcome Assessments for RMSC Clients
by Sex, Marital Status, Number of Children, and Service

	Some Results	Important Results	No Action	Client Stopped	Worked Stopped	No Follow Up	No Data	Number
Sex								
Female	30.7	9.8	32.5	12.4	5.1	5.5	4.0	2078
Male	23.3	5.8	42.3	10.9	4.4	9.1	4.3	892
UNK	25.5	3.6	41.8	12.7	7.3	3.6	5.5	55
Marital Status								
Married	33.3	11.1	26.4	12.9	5.9	7.9	2.7	808
Separated[a]	38.0	12.0	23.6	12.0	5.7	6.8	3.5	724
Never married	26.2	7.2	39.1	9.1	4.2	10.5	3.6	637
UNK								
Number of children								
None	22.4	9.1	35.4	10.6	4.1	13.4	5.0	604
1	26.7	11.5	29.6	13.9	5.1	10.7	2.7	375
2	36.8	9.3	29.1	11.5	5.3	4.8	3.2	375
3	35.4	10.5	29.9	11.2	5.8	5.8	1.4	294
4+	40.1	11.3	24.9	10.8	5.8	3.8	3.1	638
Service								
Employment	15.8	7.5	47.0	10.0	3.1	13.5	3.1	1223
Legal	31.8	7.9	30.7	11.2	6.0	3.0	9.4	267
Social Service	40.3	9.7	25.9	13.5	6.4	0.7	3.5	1222
Other	33.2	9.8	27.8	16.6	5.9	2.4	4.4	205
UNK	18.5	5.6	41.7	9.3	5.6	10.2	9.3	108
All clients	859	257	1075	361	150	198	125	3025
Percentage of clients	28.4	8.5	35.5	11.9	5.0	6.5	4.1	99.9

[a]Includes widowed and divorced.

women can be distinguished from those with other outcomes (see Table 13). Proportionately more women than men are in this positive outcome group and more married and separated people than single ones. The larger the number of children in the family, the more likely it is that there were positive results. Those who were first sent to Social Service had almost twice as high a percentage of good outcomes as those who went to the Employment Service. The most powerful indicator of positive results was the number of contacts the client had with the Center, as is shown in Table 14.

A familiar set of characteristics is emerging: The people with the most contacts, a high percentage of them women with children; people with multiple problems; and those who were seen in the Social Service unit. These people—the

Table 14
Clients with Positive Outcomes
by Number of Contacts with RMSC

Number of Contacts	Number of Clients	Percent of Clients with	
		Important Results	Some Results
1–2	1065	4.6	16.9
3–9	1051	10.7	36.6
10–19	241	15.4	54.8
20–180	236	23.7	59.7

problem-solvers and the buffeted—had the most favorable outcomes. It is timely to draw again on the illustrative material from the records in order to form a clearer picture of what these people expected and what occurred in their encounter with the Center.

Mrs. Perkins, who illustrates the problem-solving type, told a researcher repeatedly that she was well satisfied with all the things the Center had done for her.[2] Originally she had gone there when her husband was put in jail for nonsupport. She wanted to work but had to stay home with the children. Mrs. Perkins asked the RMSC for *resources*—someone to stay with the children while she worked and money to tide her over. The Center arranged for emergency financial assistance from the welfare department and advised Mrs. Perkins to remain at home with her children for a while. Later the RMSC helped her get into training and find a job.

Mrs. Perkins also expected *advice*. As she saw it, "I was expecting them to tell me how to make my husband support me and how to get along on that money." Instead, she accepted their suggestion to apply for welfare aid and seek employment later. She asked the Center to intervene as *advocate* for her disturbed youngster and the RMSC was able to have him accepted in a private school and into treatment. She looked for—and said she received—emotional *support* and *counseling* on the handling of her relationships in the day care center where she worked.

As each problem was somehow dealt with, Mrs. Perkins raised others for solution. There followed help in sending the children to camp, occasional provision of things needed in the house, and a referral of the oldest child for a job. For Mrs. Perkins and apparently for others like her there was a good match between her expectations and the Center's resources and practices.

The buffeted clients, with even more problems and more frequent contacts

[2] Mrs. Perkins' account is based on an interview with Phyllis Silverman and on the RMSC file.

with the Center, were judged to have better results than the problem-solvers. Because the Burgesses are real people and not "ideal types" they do not fully conform to that generalization. However, the results of their interaction with the agency raise some critical questions about what constitutes a positive outcome with these crisis-ridden, multiproblem families.

Mrs. Burgess first went to the RMSC at the suggestion of her welfare worker to get legal aid in obtaining a separation. She was persuaded to try marital counseling instead. Soon after, the record shows the first of many occasions when Mr. Burgess was in to see an RMSC Employment worker, who made repeated referrals to jobs that lasted only a few days because of Mr. Burgess' alcoholism and absenteeism. On several occasions the family received small amounts of money and other concrete assistance.

When Mrs. Burgess was asked for her feelings about the Center she told her caseworker that she liked her and the worker assigned to her husband,

> but she did not think the marriage counseling was useful. Her oldest daughter who is married is making inquiries on her behalf through a private lawyer for legal separation. Worker asked her why she thought that the agency's work was not constructive and Mrs. B. replied that unless Mr. B. cooperated she saw no chance of success. As for herself, she liked talking to the worker and felt much better after each interview as she talked over things with the worker. As she has no mother or relatives here she found it comforting when the worker came. Mrs. B. said "I am alone and have nobody." She then began to cry.

Mrs. Burgess stopped coming to the multiservice center. One opinion voiced at the final interagency case conference was that Mrs. Burgess was disappointed that her husband was not being seen and that more aggressive reaching out to Mr. Burgess might have made a difference. But the court psychiatrist explained how Mr. Burgess made use of him and the employment counselor; he called repeatedly and urgently when he needed help but if he could not reach anyone the crisis would pass and Mr. Burgess would not attempt further contact until a new crisis arose.

By some standards the outcome was negative. Mrs. Burgess left the RMSC without obtaining what she had come for. This may be an instance where the consumer's stated request should have been met. The family as a whole might have been better off if Mrs. Burgess had been given legal aid to get the separation she wanted. At the point at which she withdrew, the marriage appeared to be breaking up; Mr. Burgess, unable to hold a job, was about to be sent to jail; both parents were drinking more heavily; and the children were deeply troubled.

However, support and various kinds of practical assistance were provided by the RMSC and did go part way toward satisfying Mrs. Burgess' expressed wants, as she told her worker. Other people among those identified as "buffeted" clients seem to have experienced more improvement on their condition, as a result of interaction with the Center, as Table 14 suggests.

For people like Mr. and Mrs. Burgess, emotional support and practical interventions at critical points may be the most and the best that can be done, though their children may be helped in other ways. We can be quite sure that the Burgesses will be back again and again to the Center and to other agencies. Successful service for them may consist of arresting further deterioration in their situation rather than "resolving" their problems.

The one response to people's problems that the neighborhood service centers wanted to avoid was precisely the one for which the social welfare establishment had been roundly criticized. No response. People were to be heard, attended to, cared for somehow, but not disregarded.

It should be important therefore to examine why one-third of the RMSC users had no action taken on their problems, that is, they received no service. Under-reporting without doubt accounts for some of this "nonservice" but it occurred too often to be attributed to recording errors.

The people in this category have different characteristics from those with positive outcomes. A higher proportion of men and single people are found among them as well as families with fewer children. Employment problems are more typical. They had only a few contacts with the Center. In short, they resemble the resource-seekers.

A salient feature of the resource-seekers is the sharp focus they put on their expectations. The no-action situations, in which they figured more prominently than the other types, reflect the lack of resources to meet their pinpointed requests. We refer to resources that are qualitatively or quantitatively inadequate.

Overall 33 percent of the problems identified at the RMSC were not acted upon. This percentage, as shown in Table 15, held rather uniformly in the areas

Table 15
RMSC Action on Client Problems[a]
($N = 5616$)

Problem Area	Percentage of No Action	Percentage of RMSC Service and/or Referral
Welfare and financial	26.3	73.7
Family	30.4	69.6
Employment	31.1	68.9
Education & training	32.2	67.8
Housing	33.6	66.4
Health	46.9	53.1
All problems	32.5	67.5

[a]There are 182 legal problems omitted because of lack of follow-up data. Also 109 requests for information are omitted.

of employment, family problems, housing, and education and training. The no-service rate increased in health, where half the problems seemed to have gone unattended, and decreased in financial problems where only a fourth could be so considered.

The Center staff acted on a higher proportion of problems concerned with financial emergencies, family problems, marriage counseling, day care, and camping for children. One can speculate about these areas before turning to the areas in which little or no action was taken.

The financial matters generally were emergencies that the staff was able to deal with either through immediate referral to the welfare department or through its own cash fund. The family problems and marriage counseling may reflect a positive bias on the part of the social service staff who made time available to deal with these problems. This may also have been a retreat or line of lesser resistance in the many situations in which "hard" resources were not available.

Since the Center had arranged for places in summer camps and was able to recruit children to fill these places, one would expect the low rate of nonservice that was shown here. It is not clear why the employment staff acted more often on requests for a "better job" unless these people, being already employed, had better prospects for placement than the unemployed had. But these were only 6 percent of 1000 employment cases.

Large numbers of job-seekers came to the RMSC but the staff was not able to help many of them. Of 967 cases involving employment problems, two-thirds wanted a full-time job. In half the cases the employment worker made only one attempt at a job placement, some through the state employment service and some directly with potential employers. The results are shown in Table 16.

Table 16
Outcome for Clients with Employment Problems
($N = 967$)

Result	Percent
No action	28
[a]No follow-up	29
No results; client terminated	13
No results; worker terminated	3
Some results	15
Important results	13
	101

[a]Follow-up was to have been an action, after someone had been referred for a job or training possibility, to facilitate a positive outcome or to find out what had happened.

Whether more staff or more energetic staff at the RMSC could have changed these percentages significantly is debatable because of the high unemployment rates for black people. In this situation the "inadequate resource" was jobs.

In problems labeled mental health, alcoholism and the like the inadequacy may be qualitative—insufficient knowledge to cope with the problems—as well as quantitative. What is most significant is that 113 of the mental health problems came to rest in the "no action" category.

The difficulties of obtaining resources accounts for part of the no-service picture. A staff can hardly be motivated to act on problems when they see no realistic means of dealing with them. This same sense of discouragement and hopelessness can help to explain the termination of consumer-agency relationships in Roxbury. About 12 percent of all cases were terminated by decision of the client and 5 percent by the workers.

But the nature of the problem is not the only determinant of outcome. We also must look at the characteristics and behavior of the people. Again we arrive at the factor that so decisively marks off the resource-seekers from the other types—the number of contacts with the center. Sixty percent of the clients with one or two contacts either terminated their relationship to the RMSC or had no action taken on their request. We can form a clearer picture of their interaction with the RMSC by returning to Mrs. Rogers, who illustrates the patterns of the resource-seekers.

Mrs. Rogers came to the center in Roxbury because she suspected her landlord was about to evict her.[3] She wanted the Center to verify whether that was true and to help her find alternative housing. In her first visit, Mrs. Rogers was informed about the mutual responsibilities of landlords and tenants and given information on real estate agents to contact. Soon afterwards, a home visit was made to evaluate her situation in order to recommend her for public housing. The worker recorded her impression that Mrs. Rogers "is in need of long-term casework service."

At the home visit it was established that Mrs. Rogers had a neat, attractively maintained apartment and her children seemed well-cared for. She was enthusiastically recommended to the housing authority. During this visit Mrs. Rogers asked about camping for the children, and there was also a brief discussion of her difficulties with her oldest boy who was becoming defiant and difficult to manage. Mrs. Rogers volunteered that it was hard to be "both mother and father." The worker wrote that she was receptive to casework help and that this would be taken up in the Fall when a worker would contact her.

But Mrs. Rogers apparently had no intention at this time of accepting help either with money, which she said was her main problem, with her children, or with her divorce and the question of remarrying.

---

[3] The Silverman interview is supplemented here with material from the RMSC record.

This quotation from the research interview clarifies Mrs. Rogers' definition of the situation.

Interviewer: Was that what you wanted—direction and help in getting a place?
Mrs. R.: Yes.
Interviewer: Did anyone talk about any more personal problems?
Mrs. R.: Well, the social worker wanted to come to see me but I told her I'd let her know. I was going to see about getting the children into camp but then I don't think they wanted to go so I passed that by.
Interviewer: Well, what did the social worker want to come out here about?
Mrs. R.: Well, if you have a problem with kids or a problem that you could talk about to put your mind at ease they could come, so (sic) I never called her.

Mrs. R. expected and wanted *information* (Was her landlord going to evict her? Where could she look for housing?) and a *concrete service* (legal aid in getting a divorce). The RMSC staff talked with her landlord and ascertained that he was not evicting her. They gave her the names of real estate agents and helped her apply to the housing authority.

The Center aided Mrs. Rogers in having her application for public housing approved but this turned out to be unacceptable and therefore an inappropriate resource for her. She had a sick child and the transportation from the project was bad; what is more, she had not heard good things about the place. Her sister ultimately found her an apartment. As for legal aid, that could not be provided because Mrs. Rogers could not afford the fee.

Even though she said she found the RMSC comforting, the match was not good between Mrs. Rogers' expectations and what the Center could deliver. The housing was not what she wanted; the divorce cost too much. What the Center offered her—counseling—she did not want; this is another hint that counseling can be offered as a substitute for resources that are not accessible and can become a lightening rod for the ensuing frustrations.[4] A combination, then, of the pinpointed requests and expectations of this type of consumer and the lack of the resources they are seeking explains much of the nonservice and unsuccessful service at the RMSC.

The extent to which the Center fulfilled the hopes and expectations of the various types of consumers can only be roughly estimated in relation to the schema presented in Table 12 (Chapter 4). The clearest element in making this assessment consists of the nonservice cases where obviously nothing positive was accomplished. There are indications that direct services of the type that Mrs.

---

[4] Silverman points out that this is a response to frustration by both clients and workers. Offering counseling is one means by which the worker copes with the consumer's anger and disappointment; simultaneously it provides the worker with an opportunity to handle his own sense of helplessness by "doing something" that he hopes will be of use to the client. Silverman, op. cit.

Table 17
RMSC Responses to Client Problems
In Percent
($N = 5857$)

	Resource-Seekers (1–2 Contacts)	Problem-Solvers (3–5 Contacts)	"Buffeted" Clients (6+ Contacts)
No action taken	49	38	22
Direct service	27	37	55
Referrals	25	26	23
	101	101	100

Perkins and Mrs. Burgess received were satisfactory for many clients. It is difficult to judge the cases that were referred to other agencies since the outcome is unknown. This was evident in the employment cases where 29 percent were referred but had no follow-up.

Assuming that no-action was a negative result; that direct service in general tended to be positive; and that the outcome of referral was unknown and therefore neutral, Table 17 suggests the relative outcomes for the three consumer types.

The "buffeted" clients, looking primarily for direct services in the form of help with their environmental needs, advocacy of their interests, and support, fared relatively better than the other types. More than half of their problems were dealt with by direct services. Less than one-fourth of their problems had no action taken on them. It might be said that the RMSC had given these people the highest priority in setting its objectives. The program design stated that the Center would "reach out to families and individuals who have the greatest needs but are the least willing or able to seek out or use help."

The problem-solvers, looking for counsel and guidance but also for access to a wide range of services, came next in terms of having their expectations met. Compared with the buffeted clients, they received less service.

The expectations of the resource-seekers were thwarted more often than the other groups. Almost half their problems were not acted upon and only one-fourth received direct service from the RMSC staff. Lehmann comments that the Lincoln Hospital Centers had "trouble with instrumental problems of housing and employment." As a result "the more instrumentally minded clients make limited use of the facility." His term "instrumentally minded" describes quite accurately the people we have been calling resource-seekers. Lehmann concludes that the main contribution of the centers was in the form of psychological support and reassurance for their clients, noting that 51 percent of those interviewed said the problem they had brought was solved.

To recapitulate, there appears to be an association between the ways in which people approach and use social service agencies and the outcomes they experience. The process is a complicated one in which clear-cut "causes" and "effects" are hard to come by. Even before it is clear what the outcome will be, people are forming judgments and in some instances deciding not to continue their contacts. A feed-back process is apparently at work.

One of the considerations that people probably weigh under these circumstances is the "cost" of continuing to use a social welfare resource. Presumably if the price is right in relation to actual or anticipated benefits, the consumer will maintain contact. If the costs are too high, he may terminate the relationship. These considerations are taken up in the following chapter.

6
Costs to the Consumer

The possibility that there is a systematic, predictable relationship between what social agencies produce and what consumers are willing to "pay" has been implicit in the foregoing discussion. There is a hint, moreover, of a connection between the user's expectations, the satisfaction he receives, and the investment he is willing to make in his dealings with an agency. Our task now is to explore these relationships and if possible make them explicit.

First, we need to establish that the consumer, in fact, pays a price for the social services he receives. This seems paradoxical at first glance since most services are given without charging out-of-pocket fees. Rosenstock questions how free "free services" really are.

> The seemingly small cost of public transportation may impose considerable financial burden on the poor, and where paid baby-sitting is required, this also adds to the financial burden. Systematic studies have not been made of all of the costs of obtaining a so-called free service, but they exist in most circumstances where individuals desiring a service are required to obtain it at a facility some distance from their homes. It is thus by no means certain that economic factors do not play a significant role even where direct cost has been removed.[1]

There are other costs to the consumer—the physical wear and tear of travel and waiting, often for endless hours that might have been put to other uses. Frequently acquiring services means time lost from work and wages foregone. And some people experience pain and stigma in seeking help from social welfare agencies. Most of these costs increase with the amount of travel between home and agency and with the number of contacts a consumer has with an agency. Hence distance is important in the consumer's selection and utilization of a particular service.

It is no surprise that use of the Roxbury Multi-Service Center was directly related to the factor of proximity. Almost half of its users (42 percent) lived within half a mile of the Center (see Figure 2). Another quarter of them (27 percent) traveled between half a mile and one mile to reach there. Two-thirds of

---

[1] Irwin M. Rosenstock, "Prevention of Illness and Maintenance of Health," John Kosa, Aaron Antonovsky, and Irving Kenneth Zola, ed., *Poverty and Health*, Cambridge, Harvard University Press, 1969, p. 173.

Figure 2. Distribution of RMSC clients by census tracts.

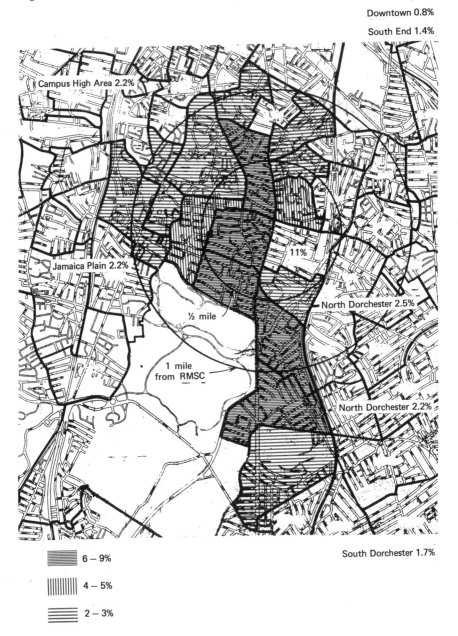

Downtown 0.8%

South End 1.4%

Campus High Area 2.2%

Jamaica Plain 2.2%

11%

½ mile

North Dorchester 2.5%

1 mile
from RMSC

North Dorchester 2.2%

6 – 9%

4 – 5%

2 – 3%

South Dorchester 1.7%

them lived in the census tracts that extend along Blue Hill Avenue, a main shopping street in Roxbury with bus routes and heavy automobile traffic.

One way to assess the significance of distance is to ask what proportion of the population around the RMSC made use of its services. The Center is located at the point at which four census tracts meet. In one of these the agency served 22 percent of the population 15 years of age and older. In the three other abutting tracts, 10–13 percent of the teen and adult population was served. Figure 3 shows that these percentages drop off rapidly in the census tracts more than half a mile from the Center. However, it should not go unnoticed that 27 percent of the Roxbury clients lived more than a mile away, some at considerable distances.

The clientele in the Bronx was even more tightly concentrated around those centers than was the case in Boston. The Lincoln Hospital centers were formally part of a community psychiatric service, but people were invited to come with any problem. Lehmann reports that they came almost exclusively from "within a five-block radius of the centers . . . within walking distance, and the existence of major means of transportation near to the centers had a negligible effect." The higher density of population in the Bronx compared with Roxbury may account for the even greater concentration of clients near the centers.

The concentration of users near the service centers reflects a similar inclination among poor people to shop in neighborhood stores that are familiar and congenial in race and language and to avoid buying in the bureaucratic, "downtown" stores, despite the fact that they pay more where they buy.[2] This was part of a more general tendency toward a restricted "life-space" that Jahoda, Lazarsfeld and Zeisel found among lower-class people.[3]

There is an interesting parallel between what Caplovitz discovered among poor consumers in New York City and what the Roxbury data show. The higher the educational level and the younger the age of the family head, the greater the tendency Caplovitz found to shop outside the neighborhood. While the tendency is only a modest one, it is also the better educated, younger people who traveled the longest distances, often from other neighborhoods, to get to the Center in Roxbury.

The general conclusion about location and utilization is that *use varied directly with distance from the facility*. Almost half the clients in Roxbury lived within half a mile of the Center and two-thirds lived on either side of a main traffic artery on which the agency was located. This does not conform with McKinlay's observation that "there is little evidence that the geographic

---

[2] David Caplovitz, *The Poor Pay More*, New York; The Free Press, 1963, p. 49; Lola M. Irelan, ed., *Low-Income Life Styles*, U.S. Department of Health, Education, and Welfare, Welfare Administration, p. 75.

[3] Quoted in Caplovitz, *ibid*.

Figure 3. RMSC clients as percent of adult population in catchment area.

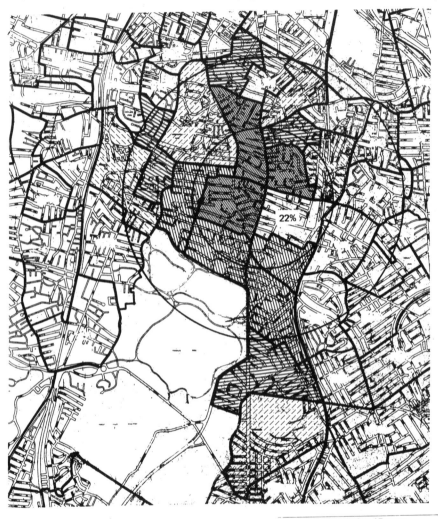

Percent of population 15 years
and older who became RMSC clients

‖‖‖‖‖	9 – 13%
‖‖‖‖‖	7 – 8%
≡≡≡	4 – 6%
⁞⁞⁞⁞⁞	2 – 3%

proximity of services to potential consumers in itself necessarily produces increased rates of use," though the studies to which he refers are mostly in the health service field.[4]

Whether the people living at greater distances from the RMSC and the Bronx centers were able to find comparable services in their own neighborhoods is not known. But the thinning out of users with distance strongly suggests that consumers do look upon travel with its accompaniments of time, carfare, and so forth as a cost to be paid for obtaining services. Beyond a certain point they are unwilling to pay the cost.

Thus far we have not examined this in terms of the consumer typology presented earlier in this study. It will be recalled that the three types differ particularly in the frequency of their contact with the agency. How did they differ in the distance from their residences to the Roxbury center?

The differences are modest but discernible. About 39 percent of the consumers who had one or two contacts lived within one-half mile of the RMSC. The comparable figure for those with three to five contacts was 47 percent and for those with six or more contacts it was 46 percent. As for living more than a mile away from the RMSC, this was true for 27 percent of those with the fewest contacts, 23 percent for those with three to five contacts, and 21 percent for those with the most contacts.

In short, the resource-seekers came longer distances than the other two groups but not to a marked degree. The distribution of problems by the distance of the consumer's home from the agency presents a mixed picture. On the whole, the differences from the expected rates—based on the spatial distribution of consumers—was again minor, as shown in Table 18. Employment, financial, and welfare problems are somewhat more concentrated close to the RMSC. Some of the family and health problems are found disproportionately in the outer zone, but not to a meaningful extent.

While distance and the nature of the problem are not highly correlated, we have seen that distance from a resource does affect its utilization. *But the most important indicator of differential costs to the consumer is the frequency of his contact with a social agency.* Each visit involves travel, time, and inconvenience and often out-of-pocket expenses for taxis or public transportation. Home visits entail these costs, exclusive of travel. Presumably the more contacts a person is prepared to make, the higher the price he is willing to pay for what he is receiving or what he hopes still to receive.

In the previous chapter it was established that frequency of contact is in fact associated with the outcome of services and with the consumer's sense of satisfaction. In ascending order of satisfaction and number of contacts, there

[4]McKinlay, op. cit., p. 122.

Table 18
Difference Between Actual and Expected Rates of Presenting Problems
by Distance from RMSC In Percent [a]

	Within One-Half Mile	One-Half to One Mile	Outside One Mile	UNK
Employment				
1. Want a job	+5	+1	−4	+1
2. Unemployed	0	0	0	+1
3. Part-time or seasonal job	+9	−1	−4	−4
4. Better job	+8	−1	−4	−1
5. Employment counseling	−6	+7	+1	+1
Family Matters				
6. Family problem	−7	+7	+3	−2
7. Problem with children	−6	+2	+3	+3
8. Day care and camp	+3	+1	0	+1
9. Discord, instability	0	+2	0	0
10. Separation, desertion	0	−2	+2	−2
11. Support: home management	−2	+11	−5	−2
12. Marriage counseling	−3	−5	+4	+4
13. Illegitimacy	+12	−2	−10	−3
Financial and Welfare				
14. Unable to pay bills	+2	−3	+1	−1
15. Needs financial assistance	+6	−5	0	+1
16. Welfare or budgeting	+7	−7	+1	+1
Housing				
17. Housing unsatisfactory	+11	−6	0	−1
18. Renter problem	−1	+4	−2	+2
19. Needs a place to stay	+6	−4	−1	−1
20. Wants public housing	+2	−2	+1	−1
Health and Mental Health				
21. Medical care	−1	+6	−1	−1
22. Mental problem	+1	+1	−1	0
23. Mental health	−13	0	+11	−1
24. Psychiatric treatment	−22	+13	+4	+3
25. Alcoholism; adjustment problem	−3	−2	+2	+3
Education and Training				
26. Training	+5	+1	0	−2
27. School problem	0	+1	−1	0
28. Further schooling	+3	+3	−1	−3
29. Academic problem	−7	+12	0	−4
Legal	−6	−1	+8	+1
Information	−8	+4	+6	0

[a]Expected rates are based on the percentage of users in each of the three zones. In the table, 93 comparisons can be made. Of these, 66 varied by less than 5 percent; 19 varied between 6 and 10 percent. In seven instances the differences was 11 to 13 percent. Only 22 percent of the psychiatric problems came from Zone 1 compared with 42 percent of the clients.

were (1) the resource-seekers, (2) the problem-solvers, and (3) the buffeted people. But what is operating here?

Do people have their expectations fulfilled *because* they persevere and continue their interaction with an agency? Or do the resource-seekers find their hopes frustrated *because* they do not invest the necessary time and effort over a sufficiently long period of time, so that a self-fulfilling mechanism works to defeat them? Or are the demands of certain consumers such that social agencies cannot provide the desired resources—a fact that is quickly sensed by the consumers who then terminate the encounter after only one or two contacts?

Bearing in mind the costs that consumers are called on to pay, let us examine more carefully the research that has been done on how often and how long people have contact with social agencies. Much of the research has been affected by the importance accorded to "continuance" in social casework and psychotherapy, as reflected in Ripple's assertion that in treatment "continuance is the necessary antecedent to use of service." [5]

Levinger argues that continuance and discontinuance not only indicate the number of dropouts but provide evidence of success in establishing the client-worker relationship.[6] Since a sustained relationship is considered the *sine qua non* of the treatment process, continuance is viewed as a critical requirement. Little wonder, then, that until recently the dominant point of view in social work has been that, except for planned early case closings, short-term contacts were less desirable.

However, there is evidence to the contrary. A recent study suggests that for people who seek help for psychological and social problems from family agencies, child guidance clinics and outpatient clinics, planned short-term treatment yields results that are as good (or better) than open-ended treatment of longer duration.[7]

Briar, in his review of research on continuance, points to inconclusive evidence on the relationship between the nature of a person's problem and the frequency or length of his contact with an agency.[8] Ripple and Blenker reached opposite conclusions as to whether people who presented psychological and interpersonal problems were more likely to be continuers than those with external or environmental difficulties.

[5] Lillian Ripple, "Factors Associated with Continuance in Casework Service," *Social Work*, Vol. 2, No. 1, January 1957, p. 87.

[6] George Levinger, "Continuance in Casework and Other Helping Relationships: A Review of Current Research," *Social Work*, Vol. 5, No. 3 (July 1960), p. 40.

[7] William J. Reid and Ann W. Shyne, *Brief and Extended Casework,* New York: Columbia University Press, 1969, p. 188.

[8] Scott Briar, "Family Services," in *Five Fields of Social Service*, Henry S. Maas, ed., New York, National Association of Social Workers, 1966, pp. 25–27.

Briar questions the findings that "appropriate" or high motivation tends to lead to continuance and "negative" or low motivation to discontinuance, partly because motivation has not been adequately defined. "Motivation" is used, Briar notes, "to refer to at least five different phenomena: (a) *what* the client wants from help; (b) *how much* he wants it; (c) the *appropriateness* of what the client wants; (d) how much *discomfort* the client experiences as a result of the problem(s) for which he is seeking help; and (e) how much *hope* the client feels about treatment."

Moreover, Briar feels that judgments concerning motivation emphasize appropriateness and, therefore, what they "may measure is not so much what the client wants from treatment and how much he wants it, but rather the degree to which what the client wants corresponds" to what the person making the judgment thinks the client *should* want.

In my view, "continuance" is a highly constrictive concept when applied to agencies serving families with their range of problems and expectations. It is a meliorative term, carrying with it the connotation that "good clients" will continue for some minimum number of contacts with an agency. Those who "drop out" before that point are presumed to have failed to make appropriate use of the service.

Silverman investigated the "drop out" phenomenon and challenged the usefulness of the very concept.[9] One of her conclusions was that the agency itself can have a strong influence on continuance and that efforts to reach out to people, for instance by initiating contacts and by making informal home visits, can encourage them to continue the relationship. This extension of effort may be the result of agency policy, the commitment of a particular worker, the greater availability of staff time, workers' preference for certain types of problems, and the like.

The notions of continuance and drop-out lose their meaning when applied to services such as information-giving, emotional support, brokerage, referral, and advocacy. Their application to counseling and therapeutic casework is now in doubt. The concepts diminish the consumer's part in defining his problems and needs, which may well be met by one, two, or three contacts, and ascribe to the professional the right to determine the means of helping.

Empirically, moreover, the high proportion of clients who have very few contacts with agencies raises issues that must be faced.

The percentage of RMSC clients with one or two contacts, although substantial, is less than that reported elsewhere. Lehmann notes that half the clients made one visit to the Lincoln Hospital centers in the Bronx and were never seen again.[10] Dorothy Beck found that 60 percent of the lower class client

---

[9] Phyllis Rolfe Silverman, op. cit.

[10] Lehmann, op. cit., p. 90.

of family agencies did not return for a second interview.[11] Briar and Miller report, with respect to voluntary family agencies and psychiatric clinics, that only a small proportion of the clients "continue in treatment for more than a few interviews."[12] Fowler supports this.[13] The people represented in these statistics have limited contact with agencies that we generally think of as dealing with complex problems that require repeated interchanges between client and worker.

Why do so many people terminate their contact with social agencies at so early a stage in the encounter? Briar's comment concerning the correspondence or discrepancy between what the client wants and what the professional thinks he should want suggests an explanation. Beck states the point clearly in commenting on the closing of cases in private casework agencies, where there was found to be a "marked difference between client expectations and the services actually provided."[14]

Similarly, Overall and Aronson found support for the hypothesis that "the discrepancy between a patient's expectations and perceptions of the (initial) interview is a better predictor of return to treatment than is the discrepancy between a patient's expectation and his therapist's perception of the interview." Seen from the consumer's angle, these are simply ways of saying that when the cost of continuing appears too high in relation to what he will be receiving, the relationship is ended.

In my study, the problem-solvers and the buffeted people apparently felt that they were having their needs met at a cost reasonable enough to warrant repeated contacts with the Roxbury center. The resource-seekers, on the other hand, seem to have made a quick assessment that the center could not help them very much with the jobs, housing, and other resources they needed, and they were unwilling to pay the ongoing costs of maintaining contact.

Consumers, following the line of evidence and argument presented in the preceding chapters, adjust their behavior toward social agencies in accordance with at least two criteria: (1) how close will the organization come to meeting their needs as they define them and (2) how high a price will they be required to pay. The consumer's perceptions of these benefits and costs will materially affect his utilization of a social agency.

[11] Beck, op. cit., p. 36.

[12] Briar and Miller, op. cit., p. 95.

[13] Fowler found that "despite many sources of noncomparability, the reported rates of nonreturn to a second interview, which range from 15 to 66, tend to cluster around 33 per cent. About 33 per cent of accepted clientele is lost after two or three interviews and about 33 per cent continue into four or more." Irving A. Fowler, "Family Agency Characteristics and Client Continuance," Social Casework, Vol. 48, (May 1967), pp. 271–277.

[14] Beck, op. cit.

7
Providers' Responses

Requests for assistance with personal needs grow rather than diminish in our society and consumers in ever larger numbers approach social agencies with new and changing demands. Because of particular conditions in the social welfare field, providers of services are not in the same position as sellers in competitive markets in which brisk demand leads to increased production and shifts in preferences to changes in products.

The responses of social service providers to consumer demands are constrained by the characteristics of their organizations and by the circumstances that surround them. As background for understanding their typical responses, we need to identify, at least briefly, the relevant characteristics of social welfare agencies.[1] These are summarized under the following headings.

1. Specialization.
2. Professionalization.
3. Limited resources.
4. Inadequate knowledge and skill.
5. Lack of basic resources in the community.

1. Social agencies are *specialized* in their functions, their services, and the knowledge and skills of their workers. While it is patently true that no single agency could provide the full range of social services required by a population of thousands, overspecialization has been the target of much criticism.

For many years, there have been vocal complaints that much like shoppers pushing their carts through a supermarket, consumers had to do the work of piecing together services which were organized according to the specific and narrow functions of agencies. Indeed, specialized workers in the same organization seemed not to be in communication with each other about the same family or the same person.

Sharp definition of the functions of agencies means that people and their problems must be matched to the appropriate facility or service. Consequently, agencies feel compelled as a matter of policy to withhold their services from people who do not fit their prescribed function (that is, they do not respond to those demands). Similarly, prospective consumers sort themselves out according

---

[1] For an extended discussion, see Wilensky and Lebeaux, op. cit. See also Perlman and Gurin, op. cit., Chapter 7 on "Service Agencies."

to their understanding of what this or that agency does for people.

2. The *professionalization* of social services is another dimension of specialization. While it has brought refinements of knowledge and methods, professionalism has also been criticized as a constraint on services. We discussed in Chapter 2 the fact that personnel are often trained to approach consumers on the basis of particular theories of behavior and concepts of the causation of problems. Whether these professionals will respond to the situation presented by a consumer, and if so how they will respond, is conditioned by their professional training and commitments.

Professionals have been charged with restricting the intake of organizations in which they work as a means of enhancing their professional interests. Cloward leveled such a charge when he said that social agencies and their staffs were "disengaging" from serving the poor because their public image and self-image were being tarnished by their association with the deprived.[2]

3. Even within the limits of their specialized functions, many social agencies are chronically *under-supplied with the resources required* to carry out their missions and meet the demands being made upon them. On rather rare occasions resources outstrip demands, but far more often there is a quantitative lack of staff, funds, space, equipment.

To expand their resources, providers must depend on legislative and administrative decisions to release public funds, and the activities and judgments of private contributors. These public and private decision-makers are faced with competing demands for their resources—between social welfare and other uses and within the social welfare field itself. A growth in demand in one type of service or in a particular agency does not automatically lead to an increase in the number of staff or in the funds needed to respond to the demand. Complex and time-consuming processes usually intervene, in addition to the possibility that competing claims may be judged more worthy.

4. There are deficiences in the *quality of knowledge and skill* in coping with human needs and problems. These are technological gaps—uncertainties about diagnosis and treatment, in the terminology of the medical field—which can restrict both the number of people served and the type of services offered.

Mr. and Mrs. Burgess, it will be recalled, were referred by the welfare department to the center in Roxbury largely because the department felt unable to deal with the interwoven difficulties the family was having with the husband's alcoholism, marital discord, unemployment, and uncertain income. The RMSC staff was not able to do a great deal more about some of these problems because of limitations in the state of knowledge concerning their causation and effective responses. As we shall see later in this chapter, a steady stream of demands from families like the Burgesses can lead to a situation in which these limitations of

[2] Cloward and Epstein, op. cit., p. 626.

skill force an agency to place limits on the number of such families who can be accepted for service.

5. Finally, social agencies must inhibit their response to consumers who need or demand *resources that are not accessible or available in the communities* in which they interact. Repeatedly, this was the case in Roxbury with people who needed jobs, housing, specific health services, and adequate levels of financial support. The inability of the RMSC to meet the expectations of the resource-seekers was a graphic example.

One can conjecture that in some instances the staff turned people away out of frank recognition that they could not help them. In other situations the consumer turned away when he saw—sometimes early in his encounter with the Center—that he would not get what he wanted. In either circumstance, the consumer's demand was not met for the simple reason that the means of meeting it was not within the reach of the agency.

In his critique of the present arrangement of services and current efforts to reorganize them, Morris points out the futility of concentrating on coordinating existing services to achieve goals such as self-sufficiency and self-support, when the services cannot deliver certain basic requirements.[3]

> If jobs are the desired end it is clear that none of the services now being offered (and thus available to be integrated) can produce jobs for workers with few skills; there are no extensive day-care programs for children of working mothers at a cost comparable to the mothers' own care at home; counseling and therapy do not help the mental patient nor the ex-convict overcome community prejudice against hiring; physical rehabilitation does not reduce the reluctance of industry to accommodate to the requirements of the severely handicapped; neither job referral nor counseling has significantly affected motivation when suitable jobs are not available.

How then, in the light of these characteristic constraints on social agencies, do they react to consumers' demands, especially when demands are increasing? One of the typical responses of the agencies has already been considered in Chapter 5: *inaction* or nonservice. Another response is *advocacy* of the consumer's need through persuading or forcing another agency to respond. This takes two forms—case-by-case advocacy and advocacy on a "class action" or institutional basis. Both of these will be discussed in the next chapter.

This chapter focuses on two widespread responses by social agencies to consumer demand: *referral* of responsibility elsewhere and *screening* of applicants.

Referrals of consumers and problems from one agency to another are often for the purpose of helping people relate to the specialized service or facility that is

---

[3] Robert Morris, "Welfare Reform 1973: The Social Service Dimension," *Science,* August 10, 1973, Vol. 181, pp. 515–522.

Table 19
Referrals Between RMSC and Community Agencies
(*N* = 3025)

	Number of Referrals from RMSC to Agencies	Number of Referrals[a] from Agencies to RMSC
Employment	504	48
Welfare Department	353	467
Health	149	135
Housing (BHA)	141	––
Child Welfare	85	––
APACs	80	110
Educational institutions (Private)	60	––
Private agencies for material aid	43	––
Legal	4	89
Courts	––	356
Family Service	43	83
Urban League, NAACP	39	––
Mental Health	26	––
Day Care, Headstart	24	––
Clergy	––	99
Recreation	––	166
Other	62	––
Total	1613	1453
Number of clients	1443	1453

[a]Excludes 1806 referrals from informal sources.

best suited to their needs. Referral can also be used, partly or entirely, to divert pressure from an agency elsewhere—almost anywhere else. This second purpose—deliberately directing someone away without carefully ascertaining whether the second agency is appropriate—is another of the targets of consumer complaints.

One of the most surprising findings from the Roxbury data is that the number of people referred *to the RMSC* by agencies in the community was almost identical with the numbers referred by the Center *to those agencies*, as Table 18 indicates.[4] It is not clear, however, even from the data in Table 19, whether the people who were being sent in both directions for help had precisely the same kinds of problems, under such categories as "employment" or "housing". Nor is

---

[4] There were, in addition, 13,000 contacts made by the RMSC with agencies in the community; these were related to brokerage and advocacy and are taken up in the next chapter.

Table 20
Presenting Problems Referred to RMSC by Social Agencies
and All Problems Referred by RMSC to Agencies

Problem Area	Presenting Problems Referred by Agencies	All Problems Referred by RMSC
Employment	197	467
Family	326	227
Welfare and financial	166	283
Housing	150	181
Legal	148	9[a]
Health	131	158
Education and training	64	212
Total	1182·	1537

[a]Incomplete data.

it apparent to what extent the RMSC was serving as a switching facility, receiving requests for help from certain agencies and rerouting them to other agencies.

But the information in Tables 18 and 19 plus a reading of the records strongly suggest that many people were involved in a circular path, a run-around among the social services in Roxbury and Boston. A key feature of the multiservice center in Roxbury seemed to be working, but in reverse. If the Center was to be a bridge over which people could be helped to reach and use the large, public services, much of the movement was in a direction that had not been anticipated. In terms of the original design, half the traffic was flowing the wrong way.

This is one of those junctures at which it is useful to contrast the perspectives of the consumer and the provider. From the consumer's viewpoint, the referrals must have seemed, at times, as though they were ricocheting from one agency to another in an aimless, mindless movement. Their interest was in obtaining the help they wanted and not in the organizational lines and agency jurisdictions among which they seemed to be shuttling back and forth.

From the providers' vantage point, there were grounds for believing that the Roxbury Multi-Service Center and many of the other agencies were trying to help people to move from where they had applied for help to where it could be found. We have some knowledge of what the community agencies were looking for when they referred clients to the RMSC. Referrals were high with respect to health, mental health, and family-related difficulties; that is, problems with children, financial support, home management, illegitimacy, marriage counseling, and separation, but learning problems, legal situations, and housing needs were being referred as well, as Table 19 indicates.

Mrs. Burgess was first sent to the Center by the welfare department, which referred almost 500 people to the RMSC. One explanation is that the department felt it could not cope with her needs, possibly because it did not have the number or kind of staff to deal with situations as demanding as the Burgess'. Another explanation is that as the RMSC demonstrated its ability to handle some problems and provide certain services, community agencies came to lean even more heavily on the Center. For example, given the availability and the flexibility of the psychiatrist from Boston University's mental health program, it became known that this was the fastest route to obtaining a psychiatric assessment and was a shortcut around waiting lists.

It is interesting here to compare the referrals that reached the RMSC from social agencies with those who came through the informal network of family, friends and neighbors. Social agencies sent 43 percent of the RMSC users.[5] Of these referrals, 500 came from the Department of Public Welfare; 250 from the courts; and 200 from settlement houses.[6] Ten percent came through contacts made by the Center's staff and through the public media.

It is surprising that fewer than 100 referrals came from clergymen since a few months before the RMSC opened they had shown much interest, in the course of a survey, in having such a resource in their community. The Center staff speculated as to whether the ministers of the long-established, "respectable" churches knew the poor people as well as the storefront church clergy, with whom the Center did not develop close ties.

Originally it was planned to have the Center's neighborhood workers do a systematic job of client-recruitment, but the Center was so overwhelmed in its first months that it did not undertake such a case-finding program. Nevertheless, about 200 clients said when they entered that they were coming as a result of contacts by the RMSC staff.

If the number of clients[7] was fairly evenly balanced between formal and informal sources of referral, a different picture emerges from a comparison of *problems* rather than *people*. Seventy percent of the presenting problems were brought by consumers who came through informal channels, including self-referrals who saw the RMSC sign and dropped in or heard about it and decided

---

[5] This was markedly more than in the Bronx where Lehmann found that "eighty percent of the clients were self-referred but the majority heard about the center from a friend, usually a previous client." Lehmann, op. cit., p. 90.

[6] Between 75 and 150 clients were referred by each of the following: hospitals and clinics; the Legal Aid Society; family agencies; churches; and Community Action Agencies.

[7] A total of 1587 of the 3259 clients for whom the information is available reached the RMSC through informal channels; 260 of these specifically mentioned other clients as their source of information.

to come. Only 21 percent of the problems came by way of social agencies. Nine percent were not recorded.

Among the informal referrals, the requests for jobs, training, and public housing apartments were outstanding. Approximately half of these people focused on a single problem. By contrast only a third of those who came through agencies had single problems. It appears that people who came on their own or through personal contacts tended to be resource-seekers. The tendency for those who came on referral from community agencies was to present more problems and to have more subsequent contacts with the RMSC—that is, the buffeted and problem-solving types.

What did referrals *from the RMSC* to other facilities mean from the Center's perspective?[8] Most of them were job requests, financial need, housing, and health problems. What was the Center to do but turn these back to the big public bureaucracies that are charged with handling these needs? Another reason for referrals was given by a member of the RMSC staff who commented that there was a basic difference between "diversionary referrals" of people from place to place as a device to avoid serving them, and productive "shopping around" for the best services available. The RMSC also tried to avoid ghettoizing people and therefore deliberately encouraged some of its users to travel out of Roxbury and make use of "downtown" resources.

Referrals, as seen by the agencies including the RMSC, constituted one way of dealing with the limitations that we have cited as being inherent in social agencies—specialization, inadequate services in quantitative and qualitative terms, and lack of basic resources that characterize the community in which agencies are located and the consumers live.

A variation on referral of a person to another agency is the sharing of responsibility for service, a form of collaboration or coordination among agencies.[9] The Roxbury center retained part of the responsibility for service in half of the cases it referred to other agencies. Presumably these were instances in which the Center saw the necessity or the value of making use of some specialized program or resource.

This type of joint responsibility (or response) is often employed as an answer to specialization and compartmentalization. It is used not only between agencies but within the same agency. The RMSC had been planned so as to minimize the undesired effects of internal specialization and to promote an easy flow of consumers and of communication among its specialists. The designation of an

[8] Half of the 3000 people for whom data are available were referred by the RMSC, but only one-third of the problems presented to the agency were referred.

[9] The view that the efforts to achieve coordination and avoid duplication in the social services has masked some of the worst features of monopolies and cartels in service delivery will be discussed in the last chapter.

"anchor worker", the use of a central record file and interservice memoranda were designed to facilitate this.

Interservice activity did in fact take place for about two-thirds of the RMSC users.[10] The data suggest that this involved mostly the buffeted clients and the problem-solvers and that the one-third who received only a single service were the resource-seekers. There is some indication from the RMSC staff that informal coordination among service workers was correlated with interpersonal relations and may have increased over time, taking the form of "advocacy within the Center itself." If so, it may mean that the concept of the "anchor worker" was being implemented.

Now let us examine another response of social agencies to rising demand for their services: screening of applicants. One interpretation of the purpose of screening is to sort out needs and refer those that are not appropriate to better equipped agencies. Another interpretation is that agencies do this in order to "cream," that is, to select out the more amenable, promising clients and turn away those who are "difficult," "uncooperative," or "unappealing." This has been done through restrictive policies governing eligibility for certain services and through the diagnosis of individual's needs.

The Roxbury Multi-Service Center and other neighborhood service centers were planned to reduce or eliminate "creaming" in their communities. They were either to accept people for their own services or were to arrange for assistance elsewhere. Their experience in responding to the numbers who came to their doors is therefore instructive.

About 4000 people registered for services at the RMSC in the first 27 months of its operation. These registrations increased steadily during the first half of this period, peaked midway and then declined. From 2323 registrations in 1966, there was a decline to 1637 in the following year.

Note that Blue Hill Avenue on which the RMSC was located had been a main thoroughfare in the early 1960's but was no longer a busy street by the end of the decade. The protests of the black community in June 1967 left many burned-out buildings that were never rebuilt or renovated. The streets became less safe and the population of Roxbury declined even further with the outmigration of black and white people. These developments may have contributed to a lessening of demand for the services of the Center.

To see whether the rise and fall of RMSC registrations was related to socioeconomic conditions in the community, we have made two comparisons. One compares job-related inquiries at the Center with unemployment rates

[10]Although Social Service initiated two-thirds of the multiservice contacts, Employment turned out to be the most called-upon resource within the Center, with 800 clients and 1350 contacts. The health resources, which consisted after the first few months of the mental health unit, was the second-most used service, accounting for 400 clients and 600 contacts.

Figure 4. Unemployment Rate for
Boston Standard Metropolitan
Statistical Area, 1965-66, Source:
Massachusetts Department of
Employment Security.

Figure 5. Number of Requests for
Job Placement, RMSC 1965-66.

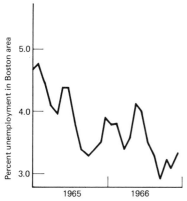

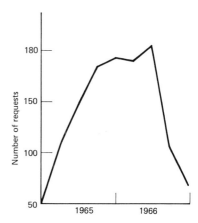

during that period of time. The other compares requests for financial aid and help on welfare problems with changes in AFDC caseloads.

Figure 4 plots the unemployment rates for the Greater Boston area; the rate specifically for Roxbury is not available. Figure 5 shows the number of people who told the RMSC during this period that they wanted a job or were out of work.

For most of this period, the rate at which employment problems were presented at the RMSC ran counter to unemployment rates. Because unemployment among blacks is both more profound and more sensitive to change than the rates for whites, one would expect the two curves to be more in harmony. In fact, the employment requests at the RMSC followed very closely the trend of total registrations rather than employment conditions in the community.

In terms of financial need, AFDC caseloads in the two principal welfare offices serving the RMSC catchment area rose by 29 percent without interruption during this period. Problems presented at the Center involving the welfare department and financial assistance increased for the first four quarters of the period, but then declined consistently for the next 15 months—against the trend of rising caseloads at the welfare department. See Figures 6 and 7.

The peaking of registrations was not related to two important indices of economic conditions of the community. Nor is it likely that other socioeconomic conditions were affecting registrations since the pattern held regardless of the nature of the problem. Several other explanations are possible.

One line of speculation about the decrease in registration is that when the Center first opened in 1965 people responded in large numbers to a new kind of

Figure 6. AFDC Caseload, Roxbury Crossing and Grove Hall Offices, Department of Public Welfare, Boston, 1965–66.

Figure 7. Number of Requests for Aid with Welfare Problems and Financial Need, RMSC, 1965–66.

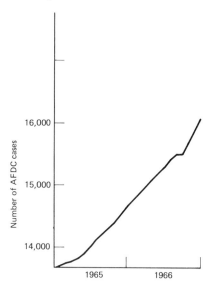

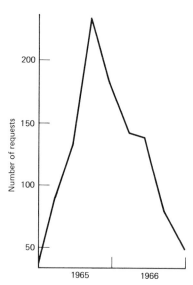

agency, a new opportunity, a new atmosphere in which they could seek help. It is possible that novelty itself attracts a certain number of people to a facility of this kind.

Another possibility is that with all its openness, sensitivity, and eagerness to be of service, the RMSC could not quickly and materially affect the supply of jobs for blacks in Boston, the availability of decent housing at rents people could afford, or the procedures and policies of the welfare department and the housing authority. Because the community's resources were severely limited, the Center's capacity to make substantial changes in the problems of many of its clients was, to that extent, also restricted.

It is conceivable that there was adverse feedback in the community from some clients who expressed a feeling of hopes disappointed. Workers in other agencies, who were referring their own clients to the RMSC with the hope that it would be of help, may also have found the results falling short of their expectations. We know that referrals from both agencies and informal sources followed the same curve from 1965 to 1967.

However, there is reason to doubt the explanation that consumers' disenchantment with the RMSC was critical in producing a decline in registrations. The very people who presumably would be most put off by talk of the center's inadequacies would be the resource-seekers looking for jobs, housing, and the like. Yet they continued coming to the Center longer than the other groups, as

Figure 8. RMSC Registration by Number of Contracts, 1965–1967.

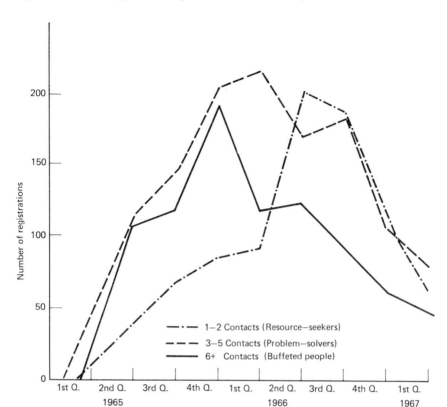

Figure 8 shows. Their peak in registrations came *six to nine months after* the multiproblem, "buffeted" people had reached their high point.

One interpretation of Figure 8 is that the resource-seekers are more active, less easily discouraged in their search. Contrary to the notion that they are "dropouts" from services, their rate of terminations at the RMSC was exactly the same as the problem-solvers (13.9 percent) and not much higher than the multiproblem group who terminated at the rate of 9.1 percent. These facts concerning the resource-seekers, who did not break off contact more often than most of the other clients and who kept coming longer than the others, belie one of the stereotypes of the poor as "unmotivated" to improve their situation.

However, there is another possible reason for the general decline in RMSC registrations after a year of operation. Could the agency's staff have become overtaxed by that time so that it could not continue at the rate of intake that had been experienced in the first 12 months? In particular, were the problem-solvers and buffeted clients requiring so much time and energy that it was necessary to stem the flow?

There is no evidence of an explicit policy decision to limit services at the RMSC on this account, but that is precisely what happened at Mobilization for Youth. MFY had originally planned to develop a "new casework" that would combine respect for the consumer with concrete aid plus counseling as a means of reducing or eliminating self-defeating attitudes and behavior on the part of the urban poor.[11] Operationally, the staff would divide clients requiring immediate, concrete services from those needing long-term casework.

After a few months it became apparent that the staff was not large enough to offer the long-term service, and workers were limited to 10 percent of these clients in their caseload. MFY then went through further shifts from brokerage to advocacy concerning "problems centering around the use of public and private agencies" especially the public welfare agency. Other problems were to be referred elsewhere and "whether a client was seen on a continuing basis or for merely brief contact was, then, no longer relevant; it was the nature of the problem, not of the client, that defined the duration of the contact."

MFY, faced with a choice of how to deploy resources that were not adequate for all the demands made upon it, gave up its intention of developing a new casework and turned from personal change to institutional change. In the process, services to people with certain problems were withdrawn.

Jones states that, "by agreeing to meet the needs of the clients as they themselves defined them, the centers soon became bogged down in giving services." "Giving service" to people whose problems do not fit the service definitions and the resources of agencies brings us back to square one. Both MFY and the Center in Roxbury felt compelled to make choices in allocating their staff resources despite the fact that this closely resembled the "creaming" and shunting aside which had been so bitterly criticized when it was done by the established services.

There is agreement among the administrators of the Roxbury Center that the decline in registrations was directly related to the buildup of pressure on the staff. Though no formal decision was made, informal measures were adopted to cope with this problem. An "informal waiting list" emerged as cases piled up. Intake workers became more selective. The staff began to recast clients' problems into "needs" that presumably were more manageable.

As the demands of clients mounted, workers engaged in other self-protective adjustments. There was a tendency for some to become more "callous" because of the unending stream of trouble and pain, raising new issues for the administrators. On the one hand, there was an evident need to give the staff support and help in coping with the overload; on the other hand, the administration, concerned with a basic commitment to neighborhood people,

---

[11] Jones, op. cit.

wondered whether the agency needed a "follow-up unit" independent of the service staff to check on service delivery.

Confronted with the complexity and number of demands being made on them, staff members resorted to shielding themselves from the mounting pressures. They extended interviews to postpone or avoid taking the next client. They scheduled home visits in order to avoid intake duty. At one stage, the administration initiated a review of 500 cases to determine their status, but so many loose ends were found that the review was never completed and the staff time was redirected to following through on open cases.

The decline in registration may also have been due, in part, to the RMSC staff's telling other agencies more forcefully to perform the services for which those agencies were responsible. In order to channel the pressure toward them, the Center may also have been less open and willing to accept referrals from community agencies.

At any rate, both the RMSC and the MFY centers were compelled to limit their responses to consumer demand. They did it in terms of numbers of people and types of problems. They became more specialized in their functions and services and this process had the effect of attracting and repelling people with particular needs and problems.

The RMSC, the Lincoln Hospital Centers, and Mobilization for Youth served comparable populations in socioeconomic terms. One might, therefore, expect

Table 21
Presenting Problems at RMSC, Lincoln Hospital Centers,
and Mobilization for Youth Centers

	RMSC	Lincoln Hospital Centers	MFY
Employment	23	10	
Family	21	15	
Welfare and financial	15	39	70
Housing	14	24	
Legal	11	4	
Education and training	7	0	
Health, mental health, personal	7	6	
Other	2	2	
Total	100	100	70[a]

[a]Jones writes that "some 70 percent of the presenting problems involved the Welfare Department ... about 40 percent of those who had welfare problems also had problems involving housing, health, schools, courts, etc." The remaining 30 percent of nonwelfare problems were roughly divided into school, health, and a miscellaneous category including addiction, employment, child neglect, emotional illness, housing, and housekeeping. Jones, op. cit., p. 456.

similar problems to be brought to the three centers but this was not the case and the explanation lies mainly in the different programs they projected.

Employment services were a distinct and widely-publicized feature of the Center in Roxbury, but this was not so in the Bronx and the Lower East Side. MFY focused its attention on welfare recipients and their needs early and made a decision to refer out many other kinds of problems. The Lincoln Hospital Centers found that they could respond helpfully to the welfare and family problems of Puerto Ricans and presumably this encouraged more and more of them to come.

As shown in Table 21, Mobilization for Youth reported that 70 percent of the presenting problems involved the Welfare Department. Lincoln Hospital found the comparable figure to be 39 percent and Roxbury reported 15 percent. On the other hand, Roxbury's presenting problems were 23 percent employment-related while the Bronx centers reported 10 percent; MFY mentioned employment as one problem in a miscellaneous category.

Agencies project their program limits and capabilities to prospective users and this becomes a screening mechanism that influences how many and which consumers will approach them. McKinlay holds that this factor has not been given due weight in utilization studies. He refers to the failure to distinguish between different types of services.

> It is precisely this failure that is the source of the many conflicting findings on utilization behavior. Either researchers have reached contradictory conclusions from studying different services, without recognizing the differences, or they have generalized findings from one service (or subset of services) to the entire range without considering possible differences in the type of service included.[1 2]

The action of the neighborhood centers in defining their functions in more restrictive terms than they had originally intended brings us full circle to an observation at the beginning of this chapter. We commented there that specialization is a fundamental characteristic of social agencies and one that has the effect of limiting the responses agencies are able to make to consumer demands.

Now it appears that specialization can be adopted as a deliberate policy of concentrating limited resources on certain problems or people and, in effect, turning away the overflow of demands which exceed the organization's capacities.

Social welfare agencies also make use of the referral process, as we have seen, as a device both to cope with excessive demands and to help people reach the specialized resources they may need. Screening is employed to reduce pressures on agencies and to insure that people's problems are within the boundaries of

[1 2] McKinlay, op. cit., p. 120.

the agency's function. Certain people are admitted through this process—in some instances they are selected because they are most amenable to being helped by an agency—and some are screened out, with or without an effort to refer them elsewhere.

These actions are taken under the assumption, implied rather than explicit, that the resources of social agencies are finite and relatively fixed and that policies and procedures are static. Another kind of action, advocacy, relies on the assumption that resources can be shifted, even expanded, and that agency policies can be changed.

8
Advocates for Consumers

More and more concern and activity are being addressed to the protection and advancement of consumers' interests. This is evident in the proliferation of movements and mechanisms such as action and lobbying organizations composed of consumers; research on their behalf; the use of the law and the courts to defend and expand consumers' rights; the establishment of public bodies with that responsibility; and the resort to grievance procedures and ombudsmen.

In that context, it has been said that one of the principal functions of the personal social services is to serve as advocates for consumers in their complex and frustrating dealings with the large bureaucracies that are typical of our communities. But who is to perform the advocate role and what strategies are most effective when the consumer needs an advocate in his relationship with social service providers? Can a social agency have its own Refund and Complaint Department similar to a department store?

In this and the two final chapters these questions are examined using the experience of the neighborhood service centers as a point of departure. The centers considered advocacy as one of their important functions and they viewed it as a built-in response to many of the demands that first came to their attention.

In this chapter "social change" and "community action" are used in the context of our discussion of services and social welfare agencies, though they have much broader meanings and applications. The focus here is on efforts to alter the quality and quantity of services given by the providers and their definitions of eligibility. This does not purport to be a general treatment of community action, community development, social action, legal action, and other forms of citizen and consumer activity addressed to social change.[1]

---

[1] See, for example, Fred M. Cox, John L. Erlich, Jack Rothman, John E. Tropman, eds., *Strategies of Community Organization,* Itasca, Ill.: F.E. Peacock Publishers, Inc., 1970; Ralph M. Kramer, *Participation of the Poor,* Englewood Cliffs, N. J.: Prentice Hall, Inc., 1969; Ralph Kramer and Harry Specht, *Readings in Community Organization Practice,* Englewood Cliffs, N. J.: Prentice Hall, 1969; Robert Perlman and Arnold Gurin, *Community Organization and Social Planning,* New York and Toronto: John Wiley & Sons and The Council for Social Work Education, 1972; John B. Turner, ed., *Neighborhood Organization for Community Action,* Report of the Conference on "Citizen Self-Help Organizations: Relevance and Problems," Cleveland, March 1967, New York: National Association of Social Workers.

Our discussion is concerned with two forms of advocacy as practiced by social agencies—case advocacy and institutional advocacy—and with the relationship between them. Toward the end of this chapter we examine the issue of the compatibility or feasibility of conducting both kinds of advocacy from the same organizational base.

The neighborhood centers were charged, *inter alia,* with the responsibility to lead, persuade, or pressure the established social agencies and other organizations into altering their policies and procedures so as to be more responsive to consumer needs. Two approaches to accomplishing this were *case advocacy* and *institutional change.* The former consisted of interventions to benefit a particular person. The latter entailed analysis of needs, planning, and the use of influence and mobilization of pressure to achieve change on a policy level. We begin with a discussion of the efforts of the Roxbury Multi-Service Center to effect changes through case advocacy.

The Roxbury Center initiated a large number of contacts with social agencies in Boston. There were 13,000 such brokerage and advocacy actions taken on behalf of 3000 RMSC users, or a mean of 4.3 contacts per client. Table 22 indicates the distribution of these contacts by type of agency.

Table 22
RMSC Contacts with Community
Agencies and Businessmen
($N = 2599$)

Type of Organization	Number of RMSC-initiated Contacts
Welfare Department	2898
Health	2004
[a] Businessmen	1563
Employment	1421
Housing	1036
Public schools	737
Family and children's agencies	726
Courts	518
Antipoverty programs	367
Recreation	190
Clergy	139
Other	1377
Total	12976

[a]Primarily for job openings and in connection with credit purchases.

Overall, 70 percent of these contacts were made by RMSC staff and 30 percent by clients. The ratio between worker-initiated contacts and client-made contacts is of interest; the former indicates the areas where the RMSC used direct intervention and possibly pressure as distinct from those areas where the staff presumably felt more confident that the person could obtain what was wanted on his own.

In dealing with the public schools, the records show *no contacts* made exclusively by clients. All 700 were the work of the Center staff, a fact that takes on deeper meaning when the project the RMSC initiated on behalf of children who were out of school is described. The ratio of worker contacts to client contacts was 5 to 1 with the Welfare Department, 3 to 1 with health agencies, and 2 to 1 in housing.

For a fuller understanding of the meaning and effect of these contacts and the referrals discussed earlier, let us examine a penetrating study by Brian Wharf.[2] Wharf's investigation was undertaken to explore how effectively the RMSC was able to realize its intentions to focus on developing liaison activities with other agencies; on identifying unmet needs; and on changing the policies of other organizations, as distinct from an emphasis on referral of clients, advocacy, and direct service. The data were obtained from staff members of the center and from the personnel of other agencies.

Initially, Wharf assumed that all staff members of the center were extensively involved in change-oriented activities, but he found on analyzing their time allocation that only a few staff members gave more than minimal attention to these activities. These workers fitted the concept of boundary personnel, that is, staff who devote a major portion of their time to working with other agencies.

The first distinct boundary position to be established was that of the child welfare specialist, who was employed and supported jointly by the RMSC and a committee of child welfare agency executives, sponsored by United Community Services, Boston's welfare council. The position was established in the advocate

---

[2] Brian W. H. Wharf, "Boundary Personnel: An Exploratory Study of Their Role Responsibility and Inter-organizational Behavior," (Unpublished doctoral dissertation, Brandeis University), 1969.

The study was conducted in the Spring of 1968 whereas this investigation covered the period from December, 1964 through March, 1967. However, Wharf's study was oriented towards the Center's first three years of operation.

He collected his data through questionnaires administered to 26 RMSC staff members and to a senior administrator and a line staff member from eight service agencies, the welfare council and ABCD. These included the Housing Authority, the Welfare Department, the Department of Employment Security, and three voluntary child welfare agencies, but did not include health or public education agencies.

mold to identify child welfare needs in Roxbury, to report on these to the committee, and to consult with other RMSC staff.

In her report in 1967 the specialist made 18 recommendations for the expansion or establishment of services involving children, for example, a program for unmarried mothers and their babies, day care services for working mothers, better programs for the retarded, and the like. The report cited case situations and noted that 83 referrals had been made by the RMSC but only 56 had been accepted by other agencies.

Wharf notes that some progress was made on the specialist's recommendations, but that the most significant change—the establishment of a Roxbury branch of Boston Children's Service—did not come about through the committee of executives to whom the recommendations had been made. He concludes that despite the failure to gather quantitative data on a cumulative basis, the child welfare specialist did identify gaps in service, did report them to those engaged in providing these services in Boston, and did document the need for the new branch of the voluntary agency.

On another front, Wharf's study discusses the housing unit inaugurated in 1966 with one staff member, partly to help particular families, but also to work with groups of tenants and to explore ways of increasing the supply of low income housing in the community. In the following months, this worker and others who were added to the unit devoted most of their efforts to what the RMSC worker called "militant advocacy" in insisting that the Boston Housing Authority fulfill its obligations to families seeking public housing "regardless of local attitudes and patterns of discrimination against Negro applicants."

Wharf points out that the RMSC supervisor arranged for a city housing inspector to be assigned on a regular basis to the RMSC and that she established a board within the Center to review landlord-tenant disputes. Above all, the housing workers *were successful in having RMSC clients accepted into public housing.* Beyond this, however, no policy or structural changes were achieved either in the Boston Housing Authority or the private housing market.

Nor was the Center more successful in changing the practices or the policies of other agencies. How did their efforts appear to personnel in the target organizations? According to administrators and workers in those agencies, the dominant tasks of the RMSC staff were client-related, a perception that conformed to the Center staff's own account of its allocation of time. The comments about referrals from the RMSC are worth recalling.

The agency respondents said that referrals from the RMSC had been only moderate in volume and had been appropriate to the functions of their agencies and the people referred were similar to other applicants. They considered the referral and advocacy activities of the Center "very effective" because of the emphasis placed on ensuring that the clients who were referred did receive service. The agencies that received RMSC referrals admired the persistence and effectiveness of the Center staff in making sure that their clients were actually *accepted* for service. But there was a rather even division of opinion as to whether advocacy had produced any *more or better service* for RMSC clients.

All agreed, however, that advocacy had not brought about policy changes. Interestingly, the staff members of the Boston Housing Authority did not perceive the RMSC activities as "militant advocacy" but as helpful and cooperative. They pointed out that RMSC staff had supplied up-to-date information on applicants to BHA and had effectively interpreted BHA rules to them. The RMSC staff had said that they deliberately used conflict strategies to obtain needed services, but the agencies perceived the working relationship in highly positive terms. They felt, for example, that service coordination had been strengthened—on an individual case level.

The agency representatives were divided evenly as to whether the RMSC had brought needs and gaps in service to their attention. However, it is important to register that the three large public agencies—welfare, employment, and the Boston Housing Authority—were among those who said they had not been made any more aware of needs. Staff from the child welfare agencies said they had, but it did not appear that they had acted on the basis of their greater understanding of Roxbury's problems. Wharf notes that the committee of child welfare executives

> was confronted with grave needs in every community in the metropolitan area, together with a shortage of resources in terms of staff and finances. Faced with this disparity between needs and resources, the Committee elected to operate on the basis that Roxbury's needs were no more acute than those of the other areas. Given their inability to move toward meeting needs in all areas, the fairest solution was not to expand services anywhere![3]

With respect to the Center's attempting, or more significantly, achieving changes in their agencies, the respondents felt that this goal was pursued less often and less successfully than the objectives considered above. "The predominant image of the Center that emerged from target agency personnel," Wharf observed, "is of an agency committed to serving the multi-problem family beset by a number of severe environmental difficulties."

The RMSC recognized, through its own experience, the sheer inadequacy of resources and services in relation to the community's needs. Furthermore, the staff experienced the limitations of trying to accomplish changes on a policy level by means of case advocacy, even when a great investment of staff time went into these activities, such as making 13,000 agency contacts.

The same conclusion was reached at Mobilization for Youth. "As the months passed," Jones writes, "it became clear that the advocacy stance of the workers was successful in achieving concrete gains for the vast majority of clients, but

[3] *Ibid.* p. 28.

was not particularly useful in bringing about broad changes in the policy of the Department of Welfare. ... By becoming advocates the center staffs became engaged in controversy, and this made cooperation ... impossible. But it seems likely that at the time the centers would have achieved a good deal less with most institutions had they avoided controversy and used friendly persuasion."[4]

At this time, MFY decided to organize groups of welfare clients to press for changes in the welfare department's procedures and policies through concerted action. This decision was made because the staff considered such action necessary in order to press service bureaucracies to become more responsive to people's needs and because of a desire to experiment with the idea that participation in social action is therapeutic for the client.[5]

The Roxbury Center, also frustrated with case advocacy as a means of bringing about institutional changes, decided to shift its strategy, but in a somewhat different direction from MFY. The RMSC began to move, Wharf notes, "from a concentration on direct services during 1965, to stressing the importance of identifying needs in 1966 and 1967, to an awareness in 1968 of the necessity to commit itself to social planning."[6]

However, the Center's lack of success in achieving institutional change, which Wharf found to be the situation when he completed his study, was due, in his view, to the failure to assign this task as an explicit responsibility to a particular person or unit and to furnish that person or unit with the requisite training and resources to do the job. He recommended that the Center devote more attention to working toward changes in the social welfare system.

Wharf suggested that the RMSC establish a unit to identify and measure deficiencies in social service programs. This would require the systematic collection of quantitative data that would go far beyond identifying needs at the level of the individual case and the direct service practitioner. This research and planning unit would specify what resources were needed to meet specific needs and would work for the achievement of its plans by cooperation where possible, or by aggressive social and political action where necessary.

It would be incomplete and inaccurate to leave this account at the point at which Wharf finished his investigation. In the time since then, the RMSC has been increasingly involved in advocate activities on a community or institutional level. One illustration is presented here.

By the end of 1968, the Roxbury Multi-Service Center had become aware that a large number of school-age children were actually not in school. The Center documented the nature and extent of this problem in a preliminary way from its own case records with the help of the unit on loan from the Boston University

---

[4] Jones, op. cit., pp. 46–52,

[5] *Idem.*

[6] Wharf, op. cit., p. 28.

mental health program. They identified those children who had been excluded because they were culturally different (Spanish-speaking children were an example); those who were physically different (crippled children and pregnant girls illustrated this) and those who were different in mental or behavioral terms (such as the mentally retarded).

The RMSC Executive Director called a conference, which was attended by 35 agencies, to present the problem of "the excluded child" and from this there emerged a Task Force on Children Out of School. The Task Force produced a hard-hitting report with recommendations for changes in the Boston Public Schools and in the State's mental health program as well as in the policies of other organizations.[7]

Without presenting in detail the process or the outcome (the process continues to this writing), one can point to the fact that the Task Force was instrumental in mobilizing enough support to achieve some substantive changes in the school system's handling of "excluded" children, the passage of bilingual education bills in the State legislature, and other changes.

The campaign on behalf of children out of school illustrates the importance of meeting two requirements for effective advocacy of an institutional nature. One, which Wharf had earlier recommended, was the technical capability of collecting and analyzing information in order to document a need. Largely through resources made available by the Boston University mental health program, information on the excluded children was gathered from the RMSC files and elsewhere and used to describe the size and nature of the problem and to buttress the case for specific objectives. Side by side with the technical ability to make a case was the mobilization of sufficient influence so that "the facts" were given a respectful hearing by policy-makers in the schools, the State Legislature, and other quarters.

Members of the Center staff, notably its Executive Director, have taken leadership roles in other community issues, such as the AFDC recipients' fight to hold on to variable family budgets and to reject a "flat grant" system. In general, the RMSC tended to use a coalition strategy, bringing together like-minded groups of consumers, social agencies, professional associations, and other interests, to mount a campaign. This differs from the practice of MFY in its early years of helping consumer groups to organize their own efforts.

From the beginning, the Roxbury center maintained its program of direct service and referrals at the same time that it was engaged in advocacy and social action, much of it directed at community agencies. There are opposing views of this: one holds that service delivery and community action are in competition or

[7] Task Force on Children Out of School, *The Way We Go to School; the Exclusion of Children in Boston*, Boston, 1970.

even conflict within the same organization; the other is that the two functions ary not only compatible but mutually supportive.

The tension between these two functions is discussed in a number of writings that show when an organization tries both to deliver services and engage in action to force other agencies to change their ways it is likely to find the two functions at odds.[8] The main reason given for this is that in order to deliver services, an organization must depend heavily on the cooperation of the very agencies (welfare, housing, employment, schools, and so forth) who are the targets of the institutional advocacy efforts. The target agencies, concerned with self-preservation in the face of attack, withdraw their cooperation at the level of services to individuals and square off for open conflict with their challenger.

Empirical support for this view appears in O'Donnell and Reid's national survey. They found that neighborhood centers "concentrate on clients' personal problems: fewer stress solving social-organizational problems than stress solving personal problems." It was estimated that the centers studied spent close to 70 percent of their time on personal issues and 30 percent on social-organizational aspects of problems in their communities.[9]

This is the more remarkable in the light of other findings in their study. They asked the center administrators what they consider to be the very serious problems in their areas, what programs the centers had developed, and how they assess the outcomes of the centers' efforts. O'Donnell and Reid concluded.

> There is no ready fit between the neighborhood problems identified by administrators as very serious and the activities centers engage in. Among the problems identified, those of inadequate recreational facilities and wide-spread unemployment are perhaps most frequently addressed—but by no more than six or seven of every 10 centers. Housing problems, school dropout problems, and drug abuse—also identified as very serious—apparently are not being addressed.
>
> . . . For more than one of every 10 problems identified as very serious, administrators say they don't even attempt to deal with them. Of these that they do try to work on, administrators report little or no success with nearly a fourth. Altogether, then, the centers have not yet found a way to effectively deal with more than a third of the very serious problems in their neighborhoods.
>
> Perhaps the most outstanding finding is the incongruence between the way administrators define problems and the way their centers try to handle these problems. First, there is much less disposition to see problems as social problems than current conceptual analysis would warrant. Further, the data

---

[8] This issue is discussed in Perlman and Jones, op. cit., p. 70; Marris and Rein, op. cit., p. 54; and Miller and Riessman, *Social Class and Social Policy*, p. 252.

[9] Edward J. O'Donnell and Otto M. Reid, "The Multiservice Neighborhood Center," *Welfare in Review*, Washington: U. S. Department of Health, Education, and Welfare, May—June 1972.

suggest that even when the administrator views problems as primarily social, organizational, or institutional, center activities still most often focus on the person—on trying to change him or at least deal with *his* problem... Perhaps there is good reason for neighborhood centers and social service agencies to pursue person-oriented methods, even while recognizing the social character of the problems. After all, it is not institutions that confront social service agencies and workers with problems—it is people.

O'Donnell and Reid did not attempt to study in depth those centers which succeeded to some extent in riding the two horses of "services and social action" at the same time. Nor did they probe the reasons for the apparent failure of so many centers to achieve a durable "mix" of the two functions. It is important, therefore, to ponder the experience of the Roxbury center in attempting to do what many others failed to do. The following paragraphs present the retrospective thoughts of the person who became Executive Director of the Roxbury Center in the summer of 1967.

Although, in his opinion, the Center was not overly effective in either services or action, what it did accomplish can be traced to several strategies. The RMSC began by first building a service program that engendered credibility and respect in Roxbury and the wider Boston community among consumers, community leaders, and social service professionals *before* it moved into social action. Most other centers began with a community action approach and later moved, often reluctantly and ineptly, into service delivery.

Social work had been the dominant profession in the Center's first two years when it was, in effect, demonstrating a new model of what the public welfare department could and should be doing. Case advocacy in particular demonstrated its usefulness and validity on an individual basis, perhaps more than Wharf recognized.

But the "social work orientation" limited the organization's ability to function as a true multiservice center; this began to develop with the decision to place service delivery in the broader context of collective, institutional action. This meant using "cases" to provide material for undertaking advocacy on an institutional level. The RMSC continued to pursue a strategy that combined collaboration and conflict in relation to target organizations such as the welfare department, the housing authority, and others.

As the Center moved more strongly into action, it redefined its relationship to residents of the community, shifting from the model of "client" and even of "consumer" to the model of "constituent." The latter implies *mutual obligations* between community and agency that are not included in the concepts of client or consumer.

An interesting example of this new relationship and of the merging of service and action is provided by the voter registration program of the RMSC. As people came to the Center for help on an individual basis they were asked whether they were registered voters and, if they were not, were urged and helped to register.

This complemented the organizational campaign out in the community to increase the number of registered voters.

Another strategy by which the RMSC was able to protect both service delivery and social action was its ability to build from the outset a broad and varied base of financial support. This included public and voluntary funds from the Boston welfare council, local foundations, and several Federal agencies that drew their support from different Congressional authorizations and appropriations. In short, the center had never been so completely dependent on any one funding source as to be vulnerable either to financial collapse or policy control.[10]

A case can be made that the Roxbury Center somehow managed to perform both the service and the institutional advocacy functions with a measure of success in each area, although there are differences of opinion on this within the staff. At the very least, the Center did not make a clear-cut choice between the two, even though there were some ambiguities and role strains stemming from the conflicting demands on the time, skill and identity of the RMSC staff. Its accomplishments may have been facilitated by pursuing Wharf's idea that there should be a division of labor within the center. Although a planning and development unit was not formally established, certain staff members acted and became known as the "change agents" or social activists, while others concentrated on service delivery. This may have eased the strain somewhat by sorting out the roles.

The RMSC staff concerned with services continued to press community agencies on individual cases, but this was not perceived as strong pressure by the target organizations. Two explanations seem plausible. The pressure from the RMSC may have been carefully calculated to stop short of totally antagonizing the welfare department, the housing authority, *et al.* The fact that these advocacy activities were not successful in changing policies, but were instrumental in getting RMSC clients accepted for service, supports this explanation of "controlled pressure."

Another possibility is that because case advocacy can be accommodated by making concessions on an individual basis, the target agencies were relatively content to do this rather than face an open conflict over policy and the possibility of concerted action by organized consumers. In New York and Boston there was a period in which welfare departments went to some lengths to increase budgets for some AFDC families on an individual basis without making policy changes that would raise all budgets.

Assuming that advocates are effective in prying out special consideration for their clients, this raises the question of whether other consumers are losing in the process. If benefits are increased for people with an advocate behind them, are they reduced for those who have no partisan acting for them? At the very least,

[10] The comments reproduced above were made by Hubert Jones in a conversation with the writer.

the latter seem likely to remain at their own level without enjoying the improved status that comes to the person whose claims are being advanced forcefully. This did happen in the AFDC program when welfare rights groups wrung concessions one by one for their members under variable grant procedures, while those who did not press their claims received no improvements.

Overall, locally-based agencies have not found it easy to carry out both a "services strategy" and a "battering ram" strategy. From his background in multi-problem family projects over the years, Geismar observes that these projects have had only a limited effect upon other agencies and institutions. "At best," he comments, "the projects carry out a measure of resource coordination, help clients communicate with them, and play an advocacy role."[11]

The issue must be viewed in a political and historical context. The neighborhood centers undoubtedly were more militant in their earlier days when there was a greater tolerance for aggressive activities on behalf of the poor and of racial minorities. Their inability to engage in bold actions to change institutional patterns and policies in their neighborhoods may be due, in part, to a shift in the political climate in this country. The stance that O'Donnell and Reid found missing among neighborhood centers receives little encouragement or support in a climate that stresses conformity and decries dissent.

But the difficulties involved in bringing about institutional change through the efforts of a locally-based organization, whether or not it is providing direct services, are nothing new. They have to do with the structure and location of power over the resources social agencies require. Much of that control lies not in the neighborhood or even the city, but in State capitols and most of all in the nation's capitol.

This is not to say that efforts to increase the funds going to social agencies or to modify their policies are doomed to failure. It does mean that these efforts must take into account the political influence that is required to produce changes in the large bureaucracies that constitute much of the social welfare field.

The Roxbury center and other locally based organizations successfully entered the political arena and achieved some limited institutional changes as advocates of powerless and hitherto inarticulate constituencies. What happened with "excluded children" in Massachusetts is a good example. These efforts require quite different strategies and resources from those that are effective in case-by-case advocacy. Both can be significant in producing more effective and responsive social services. Case advocacy can provide the support and the information on which to undertake more effective institutional changes.

[11] Geismar, op. cit., pp. 103–106.

9

Redesigning Services: Consumer and Provider Requirements

Proposals to redesign an almost ramshackle arrangement of social services are now under discussion in this country. Steps are being taken toward new forms of delivery, administration, and finance. For some people "reform" is being undertaken primarily to cut the costs of social programs. Assuming as we do that the overriding purpose must be to infuse more effectiveness and responsiveness into the services, the goal of these two concluding chapters is to draw upon the findings of this study to examine what they can contribute to the current debate.

The creation of an effective system of social services poses serious questions. Logically, the place to begin the search for answers would be with a clear understanding of the purposes the services are intended to achieve, a subject we have skirted in this inquiry until the last possible moment. As a matter of fact, it would have been impossible to begin this study with unambiguous definitions of the goals of the services, the populations they should serve, and the program elements that should be considered "social services".

There is no general agreement on these matters because they turn on basic ideological convictions. At this moment we are in the midst of a particularly sharp struggle over both the ends and the means of the social welfare services. A discussion of the issues must serve in place of agreed definitions.

It is difficult to imagine a full array of social services in an antebellum plantation, sparsely-settled pasture country, or a medieval town, because welfare services are essentially creatures of an industrialized and urbanized society. Wilensky and Lebeaux point to the machine and the factory as "symbols both of progress and of problems in human living" and develop the thesis that social services are likewise symbols of progress and of problems in contemporary society.[1]

Welfare services have been rendered both necessary and possible by the

[1] Wilensky and Lebeaux, op. cit.

processes that accompany industrialization. Chief among those are the lessening of family supports, the greater vulnerability of individuals in old-age, sickness, and poverty; the specialization of modern life; the rise of bureaucratic organizations; and the availability of economic resources to support welfare programs. What purposes are encompassed by the social services? At the most general level, writes Titmuss, they are "manifestations, first, of society's will to survive as an organic whole and, secondly, of the expressed wish of all the people to assist the survival of some people."[2] In this country it has become customary to conceptualize the functions or purposes of social welfare in terms of two main streams of thought.

One conceives of poverty and most other social problems as abnormalities partly due to temporary failures in the market economy but mostly to the inadequacies of the individuals involved. As a consequence, social services are seen as necessary but regrettable deviations from reliance on the capacity of individuals and families to provide for themselves. Their function is to reduce dependency and pathology and to reform or control the individual's behavior.

Since services are addressed to those in need, according to this view, they are delivered on a selective basis rather than universally. This is usually associated with a desire to restrict the role of government as a matter of principle. And since the nonbeneficiaries must pay the bill for the services, cost is a central concern. Efficiency and effectiveness in this context mean the parsimonious use of resources to achieve the goals of individual self-sufficiency, social control, and humane care for whatever irreducible dependency remains.

An opposing view of social programs seeks to maximize equality and security rather than individual independence and conformity. Social services are viewed as "good in their own right." They are an aspect of consumption as normal as goods and services obtained through the market. Indeed social services are those things that practically everyone needs at one time or another and that are simply not available through the market.

This second formulation avoids administrative discretion in structuring and delivering services and stresses a universal rather than a selective approach. In practice, social programs built on this principle actually serve to redistribute goods and services in favor of the poor. "Cost," then, is not something to be kept to a bare minimum, but is a legitimate mechanism for evening out inequities that are inherent, not accidental or temporary, in the workings of a capitalist economy.

These two sets of ideas appear in the substance and the rhetoric of the struggle that is now going on to determine the size, the shape, and the purposes of the

[2] Richard M. Titmuss, *Essays on the Welfare State,* Chapter 2, "The Social Division of Welfare," Beacon Press, Boston, 1969, p. 39.

social services.[3] But while these formulations are analytically useful, they oversimplify the realities of our social programs. Their purposes and instrumentalities are the result of compromises worked out through the political process among various interest groups. This is reflected, for example, in the long litany of goal statements in social welfare. One of their characteristics is the great discrepancy among them in the sharpness and specificity with which objectives are proposed. Consider the following sample statements of what the services should accomplish.

Equality of opportunity and equality of conditions.

Reduce the incidence of births out of wedlock.

Strengthen family life.

Combat dependency by assisting individuals to realize their full capacity for self-support and independent living.

Protect adults in danger of neglect, abuse or exploitation.

Attempts are now being made to recast and reduce goal statements into more precise formulations for the reason that clarifying the objectives of the services will provide guidance for planning a more effective, rational, and economical system. Morris offers a significant effort of this type in a critique of the deficiencies of the present arrangements and in his proposal for a reorganization of services.[4] He selects "functional independence" as a central focus for the social services.

The current efforts at welfare reform have as goals the restoration of economic self-sufficiency and the maintenance of functional self-sufficiency in cases where employment is not feasible. Given that economic self-sufficiency is less dependent upon social services than upon the functioning of economic forces far beyond the reach of the social services program, it seems unrealistic to assign to the social services a goal so dominated by economic forces. However there can be constructed a viable model that has as its objective for the social services the maintenance or the restoration of functional independence for all persons. Functional independence means the capacity to take care of one's own affairs to the extent that physical conditions permit and to the extent that economic conditions permit.

Morris suggests that this objective will describe a population at risk that in

[3] Rein has further refined these formulations into four views of the service recipient: as a *customer* in a supply and demand market situation; as a *client* or patient who is the object of a helping process; as a helpless and deprived *victim* in need of care; and as the *deviant* who must be brought under control by the community. Martin Rein, *Social Policy*, p. 50.

[4] Morris, op. cit., pp. 515–522.

turn will help to delimit a system of services. The target population would include persons in conflict with the law; those with educational or occupational disability; those with physical or mental disability; children living with families under conditions of severe social disability; and the aged.

This approach would replace the present organization according to fields of service or professional jurisdiction, for example, corrections, vocational rehabilitation, child welfare, and so forth, with a structure based on functions that cut across the traditional lines. He identifies six such activities that can contribute to enhancing the functional independence of the groups noted above: assessment and counseling; environmental arrangements; training, education, and equipment; protective and legal services; liaison; and transportation.

The value of Morris' approach is that it moves beyond global and often vague goals and defines program instrumentalities that are related to a specific purpose. But functional independence is only one way of defining the goals of the social services. We are forced back again to the differing value premises and assumptions on which goal formulations ultimately rest. One way of recalling this is to present briefly a spectrum of objectives that will probably continue to influence the form and operations of the social services.

At one extreme, there is the "hard-line" objective of reforming the poor and the deviant. Next, there is the goal of "getting people off welfare" in order to reduce public expenditures and save taxes. In the middle of the spectrum is the objective of promoting independence and self-care, usually advanced to enhance the satisfaction and dignity of the individuals involved and if possible to reduce their economic dependency on society.

At the other end of the spectrum are goals that can be inferred from the statements and behavior of consumers. In this study we have seen the strivings of people who want material or economic sufficiency, that is, a standard of living that closes the gap between the goods and services they receive and those of consumers above the poverty line, whether that line is defined in terms of some absolute quantity or as a percentage point on the income distribution curve. For some, this meant access to jobs that will buy the consumption goods they want; for others it means full or partial financial support and/or the provision of goods in kind.

Another goal of consumers, also reflected in the problems presented to the neighborhood centers, is protection of their rights. This has, in recent years, extended beyond a simple assurance that they will be given the things to which they are entitled under existing laws and regulations. The aim of increasing numbers of people is for a tangible and substantial share in decision-making that affects their well-being and a voice in control of the resources involved. Still other people reported on in this study sought relief from the personal stress and pain present in their living arrangements and their family relationships.

Which points in this spectrum of purposes will be the most controlling in shaping the social services? The answer lies in the outcome of the political processes of the next few years and in the relative strength of constituencies who favor one goal or another. This is not to deny the value of approaches, such as that of Morris, to devise systems of services—not necessarily a single system—that are rationally related to specific objectives. The critical point is that the criteria for judging "success," "effectiveness," and "efficiency" all depend on the underlying values, premises, and preferences.

What "works" effectively must not be assessed only in terms of monetary cost or whether people are moved from dependency to self-support. The wants of consumers, especially poor ones, must have equal status with other objectives. A decent, rat-free home; relief from feelings of frustration and anxiety; assurance of legal entitlements—these also become criteria for evaluating effectiveness in services.

There must be elements in the service system addressed to such major objectives as self-sufficiency; protection of society from overtly dangerous persons; decent support for people who cannot or should not enter the labor market; protection of individuals' rights, and relief of their personal distress; and a share in decision-making that affects their well-being.

Providers and consumers have different perspectives on proposals to reorganize services, because their interests and requirements are dissimilar. The remainder of this chapter considers their agendas, so to speak, and their points of convergence as well as difference. Understanding the constraints and objectives of each should be useful in considering new designs for services. We begin with the services providers.

The principal constraints that shape social agencies and their programs can be discussed in terms of these factors: (1) financial support and legitimation are provided—and therefore limited—by public and private sources outside the organization. (2) the will to survive that is typical of organizations. (3) the strong tendency in social welfare toward specialization and professionalization.

Social agencies, like Janus, are oriented in two directions—toward their consumers, but more compellingly toward their sources of support. They are dependent on the Congress, State, and local bodies that vote appropriations and/or on people who voluntarily contribute money and time. These sources provide not only the funds, but usually the franchise that legitimates their function and defines the domain in which they operate.

The resources available to service providers are limited and unstable because their supporters continually have to choose among competing appeals for the use of their funds and for their stamp of approval. Since, in the short run at least, providers must work within available resources, their responses to consumers' demands (as we observed in Chapter 8) must be kept within those limits. It is possible to seek additional resources, but this is far more difficult than limiting services by responding to only a portion of the demands being presented to them. This dynamic was at work over and over again in the experience of the neighborhood centers and in the agencies they tried to influence.

The "creaming" of clients, "diversionary referrals," the devices the staff used to avoid facing the requests of people seeking help, the resort to tight definitions of eligibility and responsibility—all these are efforts of providers to limit their response in the face of demands that seem about to overwhelm their resources. There is a clear conflict of interest here between providers and consumers.

Social agencies are no exception to the first rule of formal organizations—the impulse to survive, to maintain the autonomy and integrity of the structure itself. Their heavy dependence on outside sources of support makes them very sensitive to their sponsors and supporters and less so to their consumers. In the complex structure of Federal, State, and local hierarchies in the public sector and in the relationships among voluntary agencies, those who furnish funds tend to determine policies. This accounts, in part, for what appears to those at the operating level as the rigidities of rules and regulations set by those above them.

Providers are placed in an uncertain position in which their supporters periodically reassess and change their allocation of funds. It is understandable therefore that they strive to *defend* their domains in order to insure a continuing flow of funds and on occasion to *expand* their operations into the domain of other organizations. The results can be competition and conflict unless, as we shall observe in the final chapter, this possibility is jointly controlled and avoided.

Organizations experience strains when they attempt to carry out functions that are at best competitive and at worst incompatible. This is true for both internal and external reasons. Components that are designed to achieve different objectives compete for influence and resources within the organization and for support from outside.[5] One element or another achieves ascendancy in this competition, at least for a while. Looking outward, organizations tend to avoid those functions and activities that are productive of conflict that may jeopardize their support.

The constraints and pressures noted make plausible the providers' tendency to hold onto whatever decision-making they can control in the face of the authority of supporters, the strains between the bureaucratic and the professional tendencies within the organization, and the demands of consumers for a voice in policy-making. Administrators and their boards of directors argue that they must be capable of determining how to deploy their resources if they are to balance all the pressures upon them.

Providers are constrained to function within the expectations set by their supporters. Different ideological commitments and purposes are espoused by

[5] This issue is discussed in an analysis of neighborhood centers: Jacob L. Wank, "Neighborhood Centers: Social Welfare's Peculiar Institution," unpublished paper, Brandeis University, 1970, pp.57 and ff.

supporters and transmitted to their agents who administer and deliver programs. Agencies have been established and funded incrementally, in fits and starts, sometimes in response to the "discovery" of a particular form of human suffering; sometimes to control unrest and the threat of disorder; sometimes to make society more humane and caring. Some sponsors of services have been religious, ethnic and racial groups who support them partly because they contribute to group solidarity and identification.

Operationally, service agencies are addressed to what are conceived as *problems* for the individual or society—mental illness, financial destitution; unemployment; illegitimacy. It was, of course, the division of the field of social welfare into such specialized organizations that was so bitterly criticized by consumers and their spokesman in the 1960's for being oblivious to the person as a whole and of his multiple, interrelated needs and problems. The findings of this study point out that while some consumers present multiple problems, many do not and for them this criticism is less significant. Increasingly, as in the Morris proposal cited earlier, problem-orientation is redefined in terms of a *population at risk or a target group*, whose present or potential condition is of concern to them and/or to the community.

Nevertheless, whether in terms of problems or populations, there have always been strong pressures toward specialization in social welfare and this needs to be recognized. These pressures stem from several sources. They come from consumers, some of whom limit and focus *their* requests for assistance, for example, groups of handicapped people and their families who want public attention and action drawn to their specific needs. Voluntary contributors and legislators often respond to these sharply-focussed appeals for both political and humanitarian reasons and furnish funds to agencies accordingly.

The pull toward specialization also comes from service personnel within provider organizations. Although the pendulum swings back and forth between the desirability of having specialized or generalist practitioners in the human services, the pressure to develop special competence and skill is powerful. The growth of specialization in the form of professionalism in social welfare has been dramatic among physicians and nurses, social workers, psychologists, rehabilitation workers, and many others. Sometimes in harmony with their employers and administrators, sometimes in conflict with them, professionals work assiduously to delineate and defend the boundaries of their professional turf. In some circumstances, this can correspond to the consumer's desire for effective help with his problems. In other circumstances, rigid professional lines can thwart the flexibility and responsiveness that consumers demand. Unions and civil service regulations have as their main and manifest purpose protecting the interests and rights of service personnel. They often reinforce the lines of specialization according to levels of experience, competence, and type of training.

But specialization, often cast as the Devil under the label of "fragmentation" and "lack of coordination," also has its virtues. It affords opportunities to develop skills that are tailored to a particular task. The people engaged in the same or similar tasks in the human services, motivated by both self-interest and altruism, focus on its special requirements and are drawn toward study, training, research, and technological improvements.

Providers of services are constrained, then, by the limited resources and the purposes of their supporters and by the tendencies toward survival and specialization that are pressed upon them from without and from within their own ranks.

Turning now to the consumer, we have cited some of their general purposes: material sufficiency, protection of their rights and a voice in decisions; and relief from personal stress. But these are less useful in considering the structure of services than the middle-range objectives to which this study has drawn attention. These can be summarized under four headings: accessibility; accountability; choice; and responsiveness.

Accessibility. The response to the neighborhood service centers demonstrated that there was a log-jam of unresolved problems between the residents of poor neighborhoods and community agencies and that people would come to a facility located in their neighborhood which offered to help them. The consumers' interest here is in bringing services into more timely and helpful contact with people who want to use them.

Accountability. The centers were founded on the assumption and the hope that all who came would be served and served effectively. However, some were not served at all; some were given only ineffective services; and some were in fact helped. The lack of effectiveness in many instances can be traced to discrepancies between consumers' demands and the lack of resources with which to meet them. This was especially true when the needed resources were basic provisions such as jobs, housing, and adequate income. The inability to deliver on these explained in large part why so many problems ended in oblivion and why so many people remained in poverty.

From the consumer's perspective, accountability means holding providers responsible for delivering the assistance the consumers want. In the consumer's eyes efficiency means meeting his wants at a *minimum cost to him* in time, stigma, monetary expense, and pain. A critical question is how consumers' lists of wants compare with the supporters' and providers' purposes, ideological convictions, willingness to part with resources, and technical know-how.

Responsiveness. Change is an important factor for both supporters and providers. Consumers' wants presumably are one source of these changes. But we have observed that the neighborhood centers, functioning as consumer advocates, had only limited success in persuading or pressuring other community agencies to adopt new policies and practices to meet consumers' demands. Some centers, as creatures of Community Action Programs, shared in the ambiguities of the CAPs as "queasy-public" agencies. This further inhibited their ability to criticize or influence the public social services. This sharply raises the question of how the policies and the policy-making of social agencies can be kept flexible and responsive to consumers' wants and to changing social conditions.

Choice. There were significant differences in expectations and behavior among the people who were users of the neighborhood service centers. They conformed neither to a monolithic culture of poverty nor to the stereotype of the poor as "unmotivated". Some sharply focused their requests and came to the center only once or twice, wanting information and access to specific, usually material resources. Others came over and over again, crushed by many problems and seeking protection, concrete help, and emotional support. A third group, middle-class in their aspirations, hoping to improve their condition and their interpersonal relationships, sought an array of services to assist them in their upward mobility.

These differing orientations underscore the importance of identifying what the different types of consumers want and then using this understanding in the restructuring of social services.

The behavior of providers is mainly bounded and shaped by the necessity to be economical in the use of resources that are made available to them, and to be responsive to the expectations of their supporters. Providers, moreover, are drawn by internal and external forces to become specialized in their activities and functions and, for reasons of altruism and self-preservation, to seek more effective methods and techniques. In order to respond to all these requirements, their administrators and other policy-makers seek maximum control of resources and programs.

By contrast, consumers require services that are as accessible as possible on a geographic, psychological, or cultural basis and that afford them maximum choice. Their need is for accountability and effectiveness in meeting their problems. Consumers increasingly want to keep services and agencies responsive by having a strong voice in their planning and administration.

These requirements have a bearing on how services are structured. This is the focus of the final chapter.

10

Guidelines

In view of the constraints and requirements of consumers and of social service organizations discussed in the preceding chapter and throughout this book, what suggestions can be made about the organization and delivery of services?

Our purpose in this concluding chapter is not to project a grand design for a social service system—probably an impossible task—but to discuss ways in which locally-based social service functions might be better organized.[1] By "better" we mean to take into account the needs of both consumers and providers, but the selection and grouping of functions below is frankly tilted more toward the consumer's requirements as we have described them in this study.

Functions to be Performed in Delivery and Planning
of Social Services

1. *Entry functions*

   Giving information to prospective users.

   Community education on available services.

   Outreach and recruitment for services.

   Referral to specialized resources.

   Brokerage to help consumers and agencies make contact.

2. *Accountability functions*

   Assessing the situation and the problem with the consumer.

   Exploring alternative resources.

---

[1] See the Nixon Administration's Allied Services Bill of 1972; "The Social Service Amendments of 1971" proposed by the National Association of Social Workers; U.S. Department of Health, Education, and Welfare, *Toward A Comprehensive Service Delivery System Through Building the Community Service Center*, 1970; Jack C. Bloedorn, Elizabeth B. Maclatchie, William Friedlander and J.M. Wedemeyer, *Designing Social Service Systems*, American Public Welfare Association, Chicago, 1970; David M. Austin and Robert S. Caulk, "Issues and Trends in Public Social Services in the United States," published in *New Directions for the Seventies*, National Association of Social Workers, 1973; and Morris, op. cit., pp. 515–522.

Assisting consumer to select resources and to plan how to use them.

Marshalling resources around the agreed plan.

Holding providers accountable for service delivery.

Processing grievances against providers.

Advocacy and protection of consumer's rights.

3. *Provision of specialized services*

This consists of a large number of services that can only be illustrated here:

Emergency assistance

Day care

Meals-on-wheels

Legal aid

Personal counseling

Family planning

(Services for children, the aged the sick, the handicapped, and so forth.)

4. *Planning and control functions*

Documenting trends in consumer requests and nonresponses by agencies.

Monitoring and evaluation of community services.

Analysis of emerging and changing needs.

Making decisions and mobilizing action to:

Obtain new resources.

Alter distribution of existing resources.

Modify agencies policies.

Generate interagency planning.

Institute legal challenges and "class actions."

Concert consumer and citizen pressure.

In order to translate these functions into programmatic and organizational form, we return to issues that were treated earlier in this study. How will the consumer types identified in Chapter 3 relate to these activities? What stake do they have in alternative structural arrangements? What learnings can be applied to the physical location of programs? What clues as to techniques bear on the performance of these functions?

The discussion begins with the entry functions and their relationship to those listed under "accountability." The latter are known elsewhere by such terms as "case management" and "client programming."

One would anticipate that the resource-seekers would make the heaviest use of information and referral services because of their interest in obtaining immediate help, and that they would use accountability services to a lesser extent. It is precisely the "case-oriented" characteristics of the accountability function that the resource-seekers avoid, either because they carry a stigma, because they would open these people to a general but unwanted assessment of their situation, or for other reasons.

Whether more people in Roxbury would have used an Information and Referral Service if it had been physically and/or administratively separated from the rest of the multiservice center is difficult to say. Landy's analysis of the difficulties and stigma attached to "asking for help" in our society suggests that some people who saw the Center as a source of "help" might not have come initially for information.[2] Walker's study reinforces that supposition with respect to Irish-Americans in Charlestown but leaves it in some doubt with respect to a black community.[3] On the other hand, services geared to the buffeted families would need to engage in recruitment and community education in order to reach them effectively, since these families are far less likely to take the initiative in contacting services.

From the providers' viewpoint there are reasons why the entry and accountability functions should be kept distinguishable. We have cited the difficulty encountered by some neighborhood centers when they sought to refer clients to agencies at the same time that they were attacking those agencies. Brokerage necessitates some minimum of cooperation from organizations whose services are being requested. Pressure on them to change their ways provokes self-protective reactions and counter-attacks; services to individuals become casualties in the cross-fire. In order to keep the doors of agencies open to its referrals, an information facility may find it advisable to take a less combative stance than an agency charged with protecting the rights of consumers.

Specialization also supports distinct Information and Referral units. The skills required are different from those in intensive services. The one calls for keeping abreast of community resources, changes in policies and programs, such as eligibility requirements and waiting lists, and providing this information quickly and accurately. The other emphasizes interpersonal skill and sensitivity in relation to the consumer and aggressive behavior toward other social agencies.

These considerations suggest an operation similar to a Citizen Advice Bureau in England. Kahn describes this as a facility that provides information on many subjects, for example, simple help such as filling out forms, advice on how to proceed, and assistance in making contacts and appointments.[4]

[2] Landy, op. cit.

[3] Walker, op. cit.

[4] Alfred J. Kahn et al., *Neighborhood Information Centers, A Study and Some Proposals,* New York: Columbia University School of Social Work, 1966.

If information offices of this type were to be separated from other functions, there would be advantages in having administrative linkages among such offices. They must continually collect and update a large body of information on services, many of them subject to changing Federal, State, or local laws and regulations. It would be virtually impossible for each office to do this efficiently on its own; it seems sensible for them to arrange for the pooling and zissemination of information on a city-wide basis.

Information facilities must share in the responsibility for keeping services responsive to consumers. Reports on inquiries, requests, and on the dispositions that are made of them constitute an important input in the processes of planning and development. This suggests that information offices should use follow-up procedures by mail or phone and should have a mechanism for combining their data.

Against these arguments for a separate identity for entry functions are reasons for combining them with assessment and advocacy. It is likely that the majority of the people who came to the Roxbury center benefited from that combination. The buffeted people demonstrated a need for personal contact with someone who would listen at length, help them use many resources over an extended period of time, and serve as their protectors. While the problem-solvers were as mobile and assertive as any who actively sought out services, they made extensive use of a facility that tied into one package information, assessment, brokerage, follow-through with other agencies, and advocacy.

Economic utilization of resources also suggests some form of common administration of the two functions, since overhead costs could be reduced. However, no single organizational solution can satisfy all the divergent considerations mentioned. It might be possible to have a common administration with specialization of units within the organization. As services are more and more decentralized, for example, some local units may be tilted toward information and referral activities and others toward an integrated information-accountability service in accordance with the expressed demands of consumers and the results of active outreach.

Of all the functions under discussion those in the category called "provision of specialized services" are the most varied and the most costly. They can range all the way from employment services for former prisoners to personal care of older people living alone but not completely able to fend for themselves. Without returning to the debate over goals in order to find guidelines for selecting the services that should be available, it seems productive to think in terms of a particular locality—a community or neighborhood—and to look primarily to consumers to indicate which services are in demand there. There are important realities to be recognized.

No single organization, including a statewide human resource system, can finance or directly administer a complete range of specialized services. Assuming that such an agency is likely to be the provider of basic services, the organization must develop that constellation of services that best suits the demographic and socioeconomic conditions of each area.

Alternative ways of tailoring resources to locally-expressed needs are being discussed and tried experimentally. One of these is the distribution of vouchers that can be used in place of money to buy services. Another is providing "case managers" with funds (or service "requisitions" that other agencies have agreed to honor) with which to purchase services in accordance with a plan worked out with the consumer. Still others will be discussed in terms of planning.

The needs of the three types of consumers suggest differential approaches to the provision of services. The resource-seekers, by the nature of their concerns, use many specialized services. They want to see a lawyer or a housing specialist as quickly as possible without establishing a long relationship. Their interest is in ease of access to specialized services. Given their motivation to locate and pursue possible sources of assistance, the form of organization and even the location of services are less important than the availability of services somewhere in a community. Helping the problem-solvers sort out their requests brings a worker into personal counselling, which in itself is one of the specialized services. As we pointed out, it would be disruptive and costly to divorce this counselling from entry and accountability services. This approach is reinforced by the increased use of short-term treatment methods, such as those advocated by Reid and Epstein.[5] Although they need an "anchor worker" to whom they can relate, the problem-solvers, like the resource-seekers, can find their way to and through a maze of specialized services.

Because the buffeted people require an approach that is quite different, they are discussed in greater detail. Personnel working with these consumers will spend much time "on the street," visiting people in their homes, or accompanying them to a hospital or a school. The evidence from this study suggests that efforts to "solve" their problems through psychotherapeutic methods, the development of self-understanding, and new patterns of coping are likely to be wide of the mark.

A program more congruent with their beliefs and expectations would emphasize support and advocacy on an "available" basis, with periods of intense activity when a family experiences crises. The objective is not to achieve new insights or behavior patterns but to obtain for these families whatever benefits are available for them, to protect their rights, to give them opportunities to talk about their troubles, and to offer them support, encouragement, and advice.

[5] William J. Reid and Laura Epstein, *Task-Centered Casework*, New York: Columbia University Press, 1972.

There are modest grounds for thinking that these services to people who ricochet from crisis to crisis can be helpful.

Geismar reviewed nine action-research projects addressed to these families and concluded that the results were mixed.[6] The fact that there were positive outcomes in a number of areas of family life offers the hope of forestalling serious or prolonged breakdowns that entail greater costs to the people involved and to the community. In addition to relieving their distress to the extent that is possible, a heavy investment of resources in these families would be warranted as a preventive measure if indeed it could reduce the costs of maintaining many of these people in institutions.

In view of the demands that these families make—and that must be made on their behalf—the most critical factor is the availability of the most aggressive kind of advocacy. This calls for workers with appropriate skills and temperament; it raises again the issue of interorganizational conflict with its repercussions on other functions. Perhaps the advocate role can only be performed by a free-standing organization with no other responsibilities. In France an association devoted exclusively to working with the poorest of the poor prevents these families from being totally excluded from sources of help by agencies that "cream" the more promising prospects.[7]

It is useful to note that there was some difference of opinion within the RMSC staff on the appropriate use of the home development workers who spent most of their time with these families. The traditional view was that the home development worker should function as an auxiliary to the caseworkers, taking instructions from the latter as part of a treatment plan. The opposing notion was that the home development staff should be independent service-providers, performing an active role with the family. The instance was cited of the home development worker who found a house-bound mother living with two children in a drab and dirty apartment. Noticing the children's finger paintings as the only spot of color, she expanded on this and worked with the mother on cleaning and decorating the apartment and ultimately on getting her out of the house into the neighborhood.

Buffeted people live within a narrowly circumscribed life space and are not prone to travel out of their immediate, familiar environment. In addition to providing outreach workers, service facilities for them ought to be as localized as is feasible. This raises the question of where to locate services.

The data from the neighborhood centers clearly show that utilization increases

---

[6] Ludwig L. Geismar et al., *Early Supports for Family Life: A Social Work Experiment.* Rutgers University. 1972, Ch. 9.

[7] S.M. Miller, Pamela Roby, and Alwine A. DeVos van Steenwijk, "Creaming the Poor," *Trans-Action,* Vol. 7, No. 8, June 1970.

with proximity to a facility. Beyond that there is precious little to go on with any certainty. The differences in terms of the problems that were brought by those who lived close to the centers and those who lived at considerable distances are not significant. In Roxbury a slightly higher proportion of the people who had a few problems and a few contacts with the Center came from long distances, in contrast with those who had more problems and more contacts. Whether this simply reflects the difficulties of transportation or other factors is not known.

It is known that 46 to 47 percent of the buffeted clients and of the problem-solvers lived within half a mile of the RMSC compared with 39 percent of the resource-seekers. While the difference is not dramatic, it suggests that the latter are more mobile. If this is true, then information and referral facilities can be more widely spaced than those that will be more heavily used by the problem-solvers and the buffeted people. This would cast some doubt on Kahn's recommendation that the neighborhood general social service unit "should probably serve the territories of from one to five information services, depending on intensity of need."[8] The numerical relationship between the two may be the other way around.

Thus far in this study we have carefully avoided defining "neighborhood" either in terms of square miles, population, ethnic factors, or a sense of identity and belonging.[9] The critical factors that have emerged in this study are the "fit" between consumers' expectations and what they receive from agencies and the distance they must travel.

The heaviest use of the Roxbury center was by people who lived within half a mile. There were 13,000 people in the four census tracts that correspond very closely with this circle. In these tracts the RMSC had contact with 9 percent of the population during its first 27 months. The next four tracts in terms of use had a population of 18,500 and 5 percent of this population were RMSC users. It is reasonable to suppose that if there had been another center a mile or a mile and a half from the RMSC it would have experienced a comparable level of use.

Our thinking about the location of services is based on the assumption that more resources were needed than were available to the neighborhood centers covered by this study. This is supported by a fact that stands out clearly in the experience we have reviewed. At the RMSC, Mobilization for Youth and other centers there were never sufficient resources to meet the demands. Despite hopes and intentions, some people could not be served and limits were placed on

[8] Kahn, op. cit., p. 281.

[9] These issues are discussed in Suzanne Keller, *The Urban Neighborhood, A Sociological Perspective*, New York: Random House, 1968 and in Henry J. Schmandt, "Municipal Decentralization: An Overview," *Public Administration Review*, Vol. XXXII, October 1972.

service. The service centers would certainly have required more staff if they had undertaken systematic outreach.

Applied to the Roxbury situation, this would mean the establishment of several smaller units to serve the population of 50,000 from which two-thirds of the RMSC clients came. Assuming the same type of service as that provided by the Center in the 1965–1967 period, but with the addition of outreach activities, one can speculate on how to distribute the functions we have discussed. This is indeed speculation considering the number of imponderables. Not the least of these is estimating the potential demand, for which we have little basis, even in terms of such gross distinctions as that between informational requests and intensive service applications. But, using the interpretations and assumptions stated above, one can conjure up a not unreasonable picture.

For the population of 50,000, two facilities emphasizing information and brokerage and located in central places (such as shopping areas) probably would be fully used. Three or four additional centers combining information, referral, assessment, and some specialized services—each with 8 to 12 workers—would be required, with certain programs centralized at one of these centers. This ratio of workers to population is less than that of one worker to 400 families under a French system with similar responsibilities described by Schorr.[10]

Physical decentralization would make it possible to differentiate service centers along several dimensions and this may be the key to the question of how to organize and package specialized services. Since racial and ethnic factors influence the ways that people define their needs, neighborhood centers could reflect these variations. In point of fact, the Roxbury center began to serve Spanish-speaking people and as this increased and financing became available, a new agency, La Alianza Hispana, was established in another location.

Differences in socioeconomic and demographic conditions can also be better accommodated by physical decentralization. Thus, one center might stress assistance in various forms to older people in their own homes; another would have programs for young families with preschool children; and a third would have job-related programs for young wage-earners.

Specialization of services, in terms of the demographic and cultural characteristics of an area, brings us to the ubiquitous issue of "coordination." It is now useful to consider the issue from the perspectives of both providers and consumers.[11]

In one of the cyclical attempts to counter specialization with a closer integration of programs, Boston had pioneered long before the establishment of

[10] Alvin L. Schorr, *Social Security and Social Services in France,* Washington, D.C.: Government Printing Office, 1965.

[11] Rein, *Social Policy,* Ch. 6 presents a comprehensive discussion of coordination.

the Roxbury Multi-Service Center in the development of the "health center movement," which began in 1912 and spread across the country. Its basic principle as enunciated by Boston's Deputy Health Commissioner was "the correlation of all the health and social agencies, whether public or private, under one roof, with the beneficent result derived from the contact of the workers . . . to create a clearinghouse where preventive nursing, educational and relief work may be done with the least duplication of effort, friction or delay."[12]

While the prevention of disease was one of the explicit goals of the movement, the prevention of waste and duplication—in other words, the reduction of cost to providers and supporters—was a primary target. This economic objective of coordination on the part of service providers has been characterized as "cartelization" by Warren, who describes the social services in these terms.

> They are based on the assumption that competition is wasteful and that greater efficiency is to be derived from limiting competition and allocating resources according to a prior agreement rather than allowing the individual resources of the firms to be allocated in response to the "market." The result has been a system—if this is not a misnomer—of social services which are to some extent centrally planned, to some extent the result of the entrepreneurial development of individual agencies, but in both cases committed to a mythology and set of norms and practices which operate in restraint of trade, are not sensitive to the market, avoid competition, distribute geographic sales territories, and in other ways activate a virtual cartel model in the social service field."[13]

Coordination can include collaboration among providers at the level of the client or consumer with a view to meshing programs and, assuming joint or collective responsibility, for delivering the most effective package of services, as was suggested in Chapter 7. This element of improving accountability and avoiding the loss of people in the interstices between programs certainly plays a part in coordination, but the element of cost-efficiency came to occupy a central place in the plans of the Nixon Administration for reorganizing the social services.

Services integration, the Secretary of HEW wrote, must include "(a) the coordinated delivery of services for the greatest benefit to people; (b) a holistic approach to the individual and the family unit; (c) the provision of a

---

[12] C.F. Wilinsky, "The Health Center," *American Journal of Public Health*, July 1927, Vol. XVII, No. 7, p. 678.

For an extensive treatment of the health centers of the 1960's, see Hollister, Robert M., Bernard Kramer and Seymour S. Bellin, *Neighborhood Health Centers*, Lexington, Mass.; D.C. Heath and Company, 1974.

[13] Roland Warren, "The Decartelization of the Human Services," unpublished paper.

comprehensive range of services locally; and (d) the rational allocation of resources at the local level so as to be responsive to local needs."[14]

These goals would receive general approval. But there is a hook embedded in the proposal on which these very goals are likely to be impaled. Items (a) through (d) in the Secretary's vision of integration are to be pursued as a way of developing "an integrated framework within which ongoing programs can be rationalized and enriched to do a better job of making services available *within the existing commitments and resources*" (emphasis added). This kind of integration or coordination is clearly addressed to the providers' cost considerations. Cost sets the framework not consumer demand.

Consumers' criticisms concerning the fragmentation of services were cited early in this study. The crucial points were that it was difficult for them to piece together the desired services; it took inordinate amounts of time; and the result was often failure and frustration. Stripped to their essence, these criticisms are directed at *lack of access* to a sufficiently broad range of services. These criticisms can be refined in the light of our findings.

Resource-seekers characteristically are less concerned with fragmentation as such than with getting the resources they want when they want them. The problem-solvers and the buffeted families require a number of services either simultaneously or in sequence. But, for them as well, the important things are availability and choice.

For the consumer access to resources is the first requirement. The more enterprising consumers will find ways to weave services together, as apparently the resource-seekers did in Roxbury, if and when the resources are available. The consumers who are less skilled will need guidance and intervention to arrange access to the necessary services. Expansion of resources—including their proliferation to the point of duplication—serves the needs of the consumer and *reduces his costs*.

Consumers and providers, then, have different definitions of coordination and this becomes critical in redesigning the services. Improved availability and access as well as economy have to be considered. It is important that the assumptions and objectives of a service design should deal explicitly with all these factors.

Now, let us return to organizational arrangements. There is a good deal of overlap in the financial and administrative resources needed to operate local service programs. Obtaining finances for them through governmental support or by voluntary fund-raising is a time-consuming and expensive activity that could be shared. The recruitment and training of personnel; supervision; purchasing; and bookkeeping could be furnished by one organization. There could be one administrative unit that would link Service Centers within a neighborhood or among several neighborhoods.

[14] "Services Integration—Next Steps", Secretarial Memorandum, June 1, 1971, p. 1.

Beyond these managerial functions, who will determine the policies of the service units? How will the fourth set of functions—planning and control—be carried out? One must be aware here of levels of decision-making and control: the Federal, State, and local arenas of action and the vertical relationships among them.

We assume that social services will continue to be supported for the most part by tax funds, whether they are administered directly by public agencies or by contract with voluntary and commercial organizations. The bulk of that support—and therefore the basic framework of goals and policies—will continue to come from the Federal level, as it has for some time in such fields as housing, manpower, and income maintenance.

The States—within limits often established by the availability of Federal resources—control operating policies in such areas as mental health, rehabilitation, and corrections. Local groups, in coalitions that can assemble sufficient influence, have shown some ability to achieve changes at this level. The Task Force on Children Out of School which developed in Roxbury illustrates a collaboration that not only reached out to other geographic areas but, importantly, succeeded in joining professional and middle-class support to the demands articulated in the ghetto.

The level that is most accessible to neighborhood groups—and this only in relative terms—includes those programs visibly operated in their areas with control vested in city hall, a city-wide school board, recreation commission, or a private agency. Here, they have a better chance to marshall the required influence, though this too may necessitate coalition with other groupings on a broader base.

Within the realities of this structure of Federal-State-local decision-making and control, what can be the role of consumers in the social services? The stark lesson of the past is that unless their experience and views constitute a substantial input in decisions, the social service agencies and programs will be guided more by organizational considerations than by the wants and needs of consumers.

We have observed the tendency of organizations to favor activities and functions that will be financed and to avoid those that alienate support. The national survey of neighborhood service centers by O'Donnell and Reid showed that the centers responded to constraints in their environment by subordinating or eliminating the change-oriented functions. This was a matter of survival not preference. The tendency, which is prevalent in a climate that rewards conformity and discourages challenge and conflict, is to shed the more abrasive and controversial functions that are inevitably involved in planning and control.

Hence these functions, of equal importance with service delivery, are the most vulnerable. The question is how authority and influence can be shared or divided between consumers on the one hand and service organizations on the other. We ought to have learned something from the experimentation with citizen action and participation in the programs of the '60s and '70s–the "gray area" and juvenile delinquency projects, the Community Action Program under OEO, and the Model Cities program.

A number of writers who have reviewed those experiences conclude that the impact of citizen participation on policies and programs was minimal and that more often than not consumer or neighborhood representatives were coopted, diverted, or bought off with trivial concessions.[15] Hallman sums up his observations thus:

> ... all of these programs of the '60's have essentially been comprehensive service projects in the inner city with a mixture of resident participation and coordination added. ... On the one hand, coordination emphasizes the centripetal force of community power. This is because, by and large, voluntary coordination is not very effective since the tough issues are those on which no participating agency will yield easily. ... On the other hand, citizen participation is a centrifugal force. As involvement increases, more actors enter the arena and more diverse views are presented.[16]

Hallman concludes that two organizations are needed, one for administrative control and coordination, the other for the development of citizen self-help capacity through resident-controlled neighborhood institutions. Austin reached a similar position, based on his finding that the greatest impact on institutions outside the community action agency occurred "where there was some form of adversary participation" through an organization drawing its strength and direction from the neighborhood residents.[17]

The evidence points, then, toward a measure of independence for consumer-based groups in the realm of planning and policy-making as a counter-weight to the built-in administrative and fiscal controls of service providers. But, as long as the argument is conducted in terms of an all-or-nothing, either-or choice, the solution will evade us. The critical operational questions are: which responsibilities and resources should be vested in the provider organizations, which in the residents' organizations, and which should be subject to a system of mutual checks and balances?

[15] See the Special Issue of *Public Administration Review* (September 1972) on "Citizen Action in Model Cities and CAP Programs: Case Studies and Evaluation," and especially the articles by David M. Austin, Howard Hallman, and Robert A. Aleshire.

Warren and his co-workers recently published a study that includes a careful analysis of the responses of community agencies to "citizen action" and "citizen involvement". See Warren, Roland L., Stephen M. Rose, and Ann F. Bergunder, *The Structure of Urban Reform*, Lexington, Mass.; D.C. Heath and Company, 1974.

[16] *Ibid.*, p. 424–25.

[17] *Ibid.*, p. 418.

The day-by-day operational responsibility for the performance of personnel and the disbursement of funds might best be in the hands of administrators. But in the middle area, where various devices can be developed for a sharing of responsibility with an organization representing consumers, lie such matters as the right to hire and fire key administrators; the process of budget formation and program planning; the authority to switch funds or personnel from one program to another.[18]

At some point, however, these shared responsibilities shade over the functions in which consumers must take an independent role. These are the functions that need to be performed if services are to be kept flexible and responsive to consumers. Included here are monitoring and evaluating services; analyzing emerging needs; and mobilizing action to alter the distribution of resources and to bring about changes in the policies of service organizations.

In order to pursue these functions aggressively, a consumer organization needs funds and staff at its own disposal for the conduct of inquiries, the preparation of policy statements, and the mobilization of political influence.

A dilemma arises in the balancing of independence against remoteness from service operations. In order to detect emerging social problems and unmet needs, a policy group must have access to information on consumer requests, services rendered and not rendered, waiting lists, and the like. If the planning group is completely independent it is also remote from the experience and the raw material that are needed to identify and describe problems.

Organizations protect their secrets, and service agencies are no exception when sharing information would mean revealing weaknesses or failures on their part. If they bury data concerning requests, and needs they are not fulfilling or, if they simply do not look for such information, it is more difficult for a planning group to become sensitive to developing problems or to keep track of unmet needs that persist over a period of time.

A long-range approach to this is to create a climate in which social agencies, governmental and voluntary, are required to share with the consumers and with the public their experiences and records to a greater extent than is now being done. Consumer representatives must have access to the records of service providers, along with the other powers that they have over the administration of services.

The functions embraced by planning and control, however, are not monolithic. It is inevitable and highly desirable that many forces and groups on the local scene should engage in both the analytic tasks and the action required

---

[18] It is beyond our scope to go into detail on these matters, including the thorny issue of how to elect or select the "representatives" of consumers. But among the devices for implementing their role are such possibilities as veto power over program decisions; the right to initiate nominations for administrative positions; and the right of approval of candidates.

to produce orderly change.[19] There should be no thought of a monopolistic structure that preempts the field of community service planning and action— even under the banner of consumerism—and leaves no scope for special interest groups.

One way of dividing the planning task is to broaden the base for the collection and analysis of data on community conditions. Much of the data for a system of social indicators which Moynihan and others have recommended for planning in relation to urban neighborhoods would best be collected, as Johnson suggests, for "conglomerates of neighborhoods."[20] The research skills involved and the use of computers argue for this.

But there are social problems that are not likely to be identified by city-wide data collection systems. The case of the children who were not attending school, discussed in Chapter 7, is a good illustration of a problem that was "sensed" first at a local level and documented and studied there as a basis for broader planning and action. It is a persuasive example of the value of locally-controlled resources for planning and service development.

This stance should not obscure the real limitations on planning at the local level. Despite the considerable resources that were available in the antipoverty agencies and the Model Cities programs, they were not able to accomplish much by way of "comprehensive" planning.[21] A selective, issue-oriented strategy, as in the case of the "excluded children," seems more within the reach of locally-based organizations.

The importance of the planning, policy-making, and control functions in keeping social services attuned to the needs of users brings us full circle in this examination of social welfare programs from the perspective of consumers.

We have seen that the most obvious and basic requirement, from the consumers' point of view, is that the services they want be available when they need them. We found significant differences in preferences among consumers and these differences suggest guidelines for the mix of services that ought to be available in particular areas or neighborhoods.

In addition to having services available, a second major requirement for users is accessibility in physical or geographic terms as well as in cultural and psychological terms. For some consumers physical proximity is more important than for others, but ease of entry into the network of programs is necessary for all.

---

[19] Perlman and Gurin, op. cit., Chapter IV.

[20] Johnson, op. cit., p. 867.

[21] The mutually-protective strategies employed by major community organizations in the Model Cities programs to ward off comprehensive and fundamental changes are analyzed by Warren et al. in *The Structure of Urban Reform, op. cit.*

Third, consumers want services that are appropriate and effective and this requires that agencies be held accountable for matching wants and services on an individual basis. This in turn calls for assistance to the consumer in the form of protection and advocacy.

On a collective level, programs cannot be kept sufficiently flexible and responsive to the varied and changing needs in the community without the direct participation in decision-making by consumers and their spokesmen. Hence the importance of allocating to representatives of consumers significant, clearly-defined roles in the planning and control of services.

These four fundamental consumer requirements—availability, accessibility, accountability, and responsiveness—often run directly counter to the constraints within which social service organizations operate. First is the requirement that agencies function within both the mandate and the resources that are provided to them from outside their own organization. When choices are necessary between consumers and supporters, social agencies almost invariably are guided by the organizational will to survive and choose to respond to the signals from supporters, not users of their services.

In addition to these constraints, the powerful tendency of social welfare agencies to specialize in terms of functions, skills, and clientele frequently throws them into conflict with consumer needs as the latter define them, though this may be less true than is generally supposed. Professionalization, as well as specialization, sets further constraints on agencies, sometimes in opposition to the interests of consumers.

It has been assumed in this book that the constraints and requirements of social service organizations are rather well recognized and understood, but that consumers' requirements and preferences are less well known and certainly less often heeded. The resolution of conflicts between these two orientations and interests is essentially a political struggle revolves that around priorities and the willingness to commit adequate resources to policies that give more recognition to consumer needs.

The political processes that would give more weight to the consumer's side of the interactions described in these pages were interrupted in recent years. It is time to give renewed energy and thought to those processes; a correction of the imbalance is long overdue.

Verbatim Statements
of Problems at RMSC

This listing describes in detail the nature of the problems clients and staff identified at the RMSC. The frequencies apply to 3025 clients. This information was not available on 936 clients who were referred to Legal Service and subsequently not reported on in the central record file, as well as a few clients for whom records were incomplete. Hence, the description of legal problems is understated.

In the distribution of client problems that appears in Table 19 the list of problems has been condensed to 31.

A. *Employment*
    1. Want a job   846
    2. Unemployed

Was fired, laid off, quit	74	
Unemployed	16	
Lacks experience or ability for desired job	14	
Not able to work	13	
Being discriminated against, complaints versus employer	12	
Does not want to work	12	
Unknown	1	
Total		142

    3. Want a part-time or seasonal job   303
    4. Want a better job

Want a better job	88	
Want a different job	29	
Unknown	5	
Total		122

    5. Employment counseling and unemployment compensation

Needs or desires employment counseling	44	
Not eligible for unemployment compensation	20	
Wants information on unemployment compensation	14	
Unknown	47	
Total		125

B. *Family*
   6. Needs help, advice on family problem, requests
      casework   231
   7. Problem with children
      Needs or desires counseling concerning
         children   98

B. *Family*		
6. Needs help, advice on family problem, requests casework		231
7. Problem with children		
Needs or desires counseling concerning children	98	
Adoption, paternity, placement, custody, guardianship	73	
Neglect or abuse	48	
Child won't mind or listen	44	
Other	2	
Total		265
8. Day care and camp placement		
Needs or desires day care, supervision, mother's helper	89	
Camp placement	79	
Lacks proper recreational facilities	18	
Total		186
9. Family discord and instability		
Not at home through own volition, ran away, living with another	29	
Not at home not through own volition, jail, death, foster home	25	
Unstable family environment or dissatisfaction	24	
Arguments and fights over money, children, drinking	21	
Desire marriage or reconciliation	16	
Other	65	
Total		180
10. Separation, divorce, desertion		
Desires separation	78	
Desires divorce, annulment	49	
Desertion	13	
Restraining order, complaint	5	
Total		145
11. Support and home management		
Needs or desires assistance in running home, rearing children	77	
Nonsupport	43	
Problem concerning support	16	
Total		136

12. Marriage counseling
  Desires or needs marriage counseling   116
  Wants, does not want children   5
    Total   121

13. Illegitimacy
  Illegitimacy   76
  Pregnant out of wedlock   21
  Promiscuity, extramarital affairs 15
  Incest   1
    Total   113

C. *Financial and Welfare*

14. Unable to pay bills
  Lacks or unable to buy food, clothing, and
   so forth   139
  Lacks or unable to pay utilities 52
  Needs home furnishings   44
  Unable to pay rent or keep home 42
  Needs or requests surplus food 39
  Unable to meet time payments 31
  Other   5
    Total   352

15. Needs financial aid   344

16. Welfare problems and budgetting
  Receiving public assistance, social security 69
  Problem concerning public agencies 65
  Complaints concerning public agencies 59
  Needs help budgeting   54
  Not receiving public assistance due to
   ineligibility   26
  Information wanted concerning public agency
   providing funds, service, food 17
  Does not want to receive public assistance 15
  Change in welfare status   5
    Total   310

D. *Housing*

17. Housing unsatisfactory
  Wants to move to a better place 58
  Housing in bad state; disrepair; vermin 50
  Needs help renovating or improving 10
  Present neighborhood unhealthy, undesirable,
   unsafe   16

Other	109	
Total		243

18. Renter problems
    Needs or does not have shelter; emergency
        situation 79
    Problem with landlord 59
    Eviction or threat of eviction 44
    Evicted 13
    Other 11
        Total   206
19. Needs a place to stay, looking for an apartment   205
20. Wants public housing
    Wants to move to a project, housing
        development, home for aged 155
    Was refused public housing 15
        Total   170

E. *Health and Mental Health*
21. Medical care
    Needs medical care 65
    Needs nursing care 38
    Hospitalized, needs hospitalization 23
    Medical counseling 20
    Handicapped 19
    Other 13
        Total   178
22. Health problem
    Chronic: Tuberculosis, heart, diabetes, cancer 67
    Sick 51
    Serious accident 14
    Surgery 10
    Eye care 9
    Dental care 8
    Other 7
        Total   166
23. Mental health
    Nervous, agitated, unstable emotional state 34
    Depressed, apathetic 23
    Receiving mental health care 19
    Mental retardation 16
    Unrealistic self-appraisal 16
    Recently discharged from institution 13
    Placement in an institution 12
    Other 13

	Total	146
24.	Psychiatric treatment needed or desired	119
25.	Alcoholism and adjustment problems	

	Drinking problem	66
	Role adjustment problem, rebellious feelings	39
	Drug addiction	4
	Other	6
	Total	115

F. *Education and Training*

26. Training

Would like training	214	
N.Y.C.–M.D.T.A.	23	
Total		237

27. School problem

Has problem in or with school	98	
Not in school (dropout or no explanation)	26	
Change of school desired	16	
Truant	15	
Released from school, kicked out	12	
Other	12	
Total		179

28. Further schooling

Would like additional education	85	
Wants to acquire special skills, e.g. sewing, adult education	13	
Illiterate	10	
Other	18	
Total		126

29. Academic problem

Learning problem, e.g. slow learner	45	
Wants educational counseling	27	
Extra help desired	14	
Special class	11	
Other		
Total		106

G.   30. *Legal*

Needs or requests legal advice	84	
Accused of or admits law-violation	26	
Recover wages, property, money	19	
Criminal record	17	
Other	49	
Total		195

H.   31. *Informational requests*   123

Index